KILLING BIN LADEN

Operation *Neptune Spear* 2011

PETER F. PANZERI Jr.

First published in Great Britain in 2014 by Osprey Publishing,
PO Box 883, Oxford, OX1 9PL, UK
PO Box 3985, New York, NY 10185-3985, USA
E-mail: info@ospreypublishing.com

Osprey Publishing is part of the Osprey Group

A CIP catalog record for this book is available from the British Library

Print ISBN: 978 1 4728 0408 2
PDF ebook ISBN: 978 1 4728 0410 5
ePub ebook ISBN: 978 1 4728 0409 9

Index by Alan Thatcher
Typeset in Sabon
Maps by bounford.com
3D BEVs by Alan Gilliland
Originated by PDQ Media, Bungay, UK
Printed in China through Worldprint Ltd

14 15 16 17 18 10 9 8 7 6 5 4 3 2 1

Osprey Publishing is supporting the Woodland Trust, the UK's leading woodland conservation charity, by funding the dedication of trees.

www.ospreypublishing.com

Title page image: The day after the raid on bin Laden's compound, the Pakistani military attempt to prevent photos being taken from outside the walls. (Warrick Page/Getty Images)

DISCLAIMER

No classified or confidential information was accessed or used in composing this account. All details of this account are a compilation of open source documentation, participant accounts, declassified and/or publicly released information, and – where necessary – a hypothesis of the most valid and evident premise.

USE OF PSEUDONYMS AND CALL SIGNS

To protect the personal security of those involved, pseudonyms (such as "Mark Owen" and "Pilot Teddy" etc.) are used for US military tactical participants, including those whose real names may have since been leaked and/or released. Also, tactical unit code-names and call signs have been applied to be consistent with and to match – wherever possible – the most prevalent accounts.

BIBLIOGRAPHY AND CRITICAL SOURCES

The most dominant influences on this account are those of the 880-plus-page Pakistani Abbottabad Commission Report for its inclusion of candid raw data, the personal account and interviews of former US Navy SEAL, "Mark Owen," and the abundance of detailed information on Operation *Neptune Spear* released in 2011 to the producers and screenwriters of the film *Zero Dark Thirty*.

LIST OF ACRONYMS AND ABBREVIATIONS

AAR	after action review
AFT	Afghanistan time
CF	Contingency Force
CJCS	Chairman of the Joint Chiefs of Staff
DEVGRU	US Naval Special Warfare Development Group (also NSWDG)
EDT	Eastern Daylight Time (USA)
EOD	explosive ordnance
EW	electronic warfare
FARE	forward area refueling equipment
FARP	forward area refueling point
IDF	Israel Defense Forces
ISI	Inter-Services Intelligence (Pakistan)
J3	Joint Operations Staff (Section)
JSOC	Joint Special Operations Command
NGA	National Geospatial-Intelligence Agency
NOE	nap-of-the-earth
NSA	National Security Agency
NSC	National Security Council
NVG	night vision goggles
PAF	Pakistan Air Force
PLO	Palestine Liberation Organization
QRF	Quick Reaction Force
SOAR	Special Operations Aviation Regiment
Spec Ops	Special Operations
SSE	sensitive site exploitation
SUV	sport utility vehicle
UAV	unmanned aerial vehicle (drone)
USAF	United States Air Force
USMC	United States Marine Corps
USN	United States Navy

CONTENTS

INTRODUCTION

On May 2, 2011 the world's most wanted man, Osama Bin Laden, was shot dead by a US Navy SEAL in Abbottabad, Pakistan. Although Operation *Neptune Spear* – the code name for the mission to kill or capture the Saudi-born militant and one-time leader of al-Qaeda – took a mere 38 minutes to carry out, it was over ten years in the making. In execution, it was a simple operation with just 24 men on the ground. However, in its entirety, *Neptune Spear* was as complex a mission as any can get, drawing on the full national assets of the United States. The result of over a decade of intensive intelligence gathering, analysis and planning, it still demands significant attention worldwide to this day.

Save for the tenacity of a determined few in the intelligence services, Operation *Neptune Spear* would never have been conceived, and without the meticulous planning and exhaustive preparation of many special operations professionals, it could have never been executed. Moreover, the skills and resourcefulness of a handful of elite aviators, tactical specialists and trained killers prevented the operation from quickly deteriorating into a costly and disastrous failure. Although it was one of the most successful, momentous and dramatic military raids ever attempted, Operation *Neptune Spear* was clearly not flawless.

The raid was carried out by the men of the Naval Special Warfare Development Group (DEVGRU), more popularly known as "SEAL Team Six" – which was in fact the name of its predecessor unit, disbanded in the 1980s. DEVGRU forms the primary counter-terrorism elements of the US Joint Special Operations Command, along with the US Army Delta Force. For certain missions, as was the case with *Neptune Spear*, it is placed under operational control of the US Central Intelligence Agency. While all activities and details on DEVGRU are highly classified, enough information has been has been released to provide a clear picture of the men, the machines and the methods of "SEAL Team Six."DEVGRU is reportedly divided into six squadrons: Gold, Blue, Silver and Red Squadrons are Assault Teams,

Black Squadron is the Reconnaissance & Surveillance Team, and Gray Squadron is a specialist boat squadron dedicated to maritime operations. Their multi-functional special operations missions include high-risk personnel/hostage rescue and extractions, covertly infiltrating international high-risk areas and pre-emptive counter-terrorist raids to recover or eliminate high-value targets.

In 2011, the men of this unit were tasked with the mission to eliminate Osama bin Laden, who had been tracked down to his Abbottabad compound after a decade-long hunt. Bin Laden had become the world's most infamous terrorist leader in September 2001, when operatives of his al-Qaeda network launched a series of suicide attacks in the United States using hijacked airliners, most devastatingly against the World Trade Center in New York. But Osama bin Laden's career as an Islamic militant stretched back decades. It was a Middle East war that first shaped bin Laden's beliefs, leading to the formation of his al-Qaeda organization and a global terrorist campaign, and ultimately to bin Laden's death in an Abbottabad compound at the hands of a SEAL special operator.

A crowd cheers at the corner of Vesey and Liberty streets next to "ground zero," the site of the destroyed World Trade Center, May 2, 2011, after hearing news of Osama Bin Laden's death. (Sgt. Randall Clinton/USMC)

ORIGINS

The making of Osama Bin Laden

Osama bin Mohammed bin Awad bin Laden was born in Riyadh, Saudi Arabia in March 1957. He was the seventeenth of 52 children born to Sheik Mohammed bin Laden, a self-made billionaire and Saudi Arabia's wealthiest construction magnate. In September 1967 Sheik Mohammed bin Laden was killed in a plane crash in Saudi Arabia (a fate that his eldest son and primary heir would also share two decades later). All of the bin Laden heirs were multi-millionaires.

Three aspects of note stand out in the development of Bin Laden into the world's most notorious terrorist leader. Each of these had a profound and clear influence upon him. First, from childhood he was raised as a Wahhabi Muslim (a strict Sunni sect), revering over 1,500 years of fundamentalist Arab-Islamic religion and culture. He grew up to be a religious militant and sought to express his beliefs in the life choices he made. He married women from families claiming descent from the prophet Mohammed. He also played a personal role in his family's construction work during rebuilding at both Medina and Mecca, widely acknowledged as Islam's two holiest sites. From a very young age, bin Laden did more than just embrace Islamist culture and religion. He identified himself through it, derived self-importance from it, and sought to protect it. As a Wahhabi, Bin Laden fixated on Islam's founders and the precepts of the Muslim conquest, which called for a jihad (or holy war) to prevail over the enemies of Islam. As an affluent and influential member of the privileged class and (later) an essentially self-appointed holy leader, he would later redefine and redirect such historical aspects of Islam to meet the needs of what he viewed as his own calling. Moreover, his charismatic leadership would inspire many thousands of others to join this militant and fanatical cause.

1957

Osama bin Mohammed bin Awad bin Laden born in Riyadh, Saudi Arabia

Second, Osama bin Laden developed and clearly harbored exceptionally intense and vengeful hatreds. These appear to have been rooted in losses

Osama bin Laden was deeply affected by the brutal events of the 1975–1990 Lebanese Civil War. Here, armed teenage girls guard a Phalangist milita barricade in downtown Beirut in 1975. (© Bettmann/Corbis)

suffered during crucial coming-of-age periods of his life. As a college student, his family wealth allowed him to frequently escape Saudi Arabia's strict Islamic culture and customs, holidaying in lavish family-owned properties with school friends and family in cosmopolitan Beirut in Lebanon. During these periods he developed personal relationships and deep affection for the place and its people. As he matured, bin Laden became involved with some of the religious (and sometimes reactionary) factions in the city, and he invested generously in religious and cultural causes.

Osama bin Laden's sheltered life was brutally interrupted by the time he was 18, with the outbreak of the violent, sectarian Lebanese Civil War in 1975. He felt a great sense of personal loss as the places and people he enjoyed during his adolescence were virtually annihilated before the eyes of the world, and he was powerless to help. He blamed both Israel and the United States for inciting anti-Muslim factions in Lebanon. In his mind he corroborated these views when US and Israeli military interventions followed in Lebanon. Furthermore, when the Sabra and Shatila massacres of several thousand Muslim refugees at the hands of Lebanese Phalangist militia took place in mid-September 1982, bin Laden again blamed the US and Israel. All of these wounds ran exceptionally deep. Over 20 years later, in his most famous video message following the September 2001 terrorist attacks, he still expressed vehement anger at these atrocities in Lebanon. Bin Laden continued to cite this in nearly all of his Al Jazeera broadcast speeches. He stated in 2004: "The events that affected my soul in a direct way started in 1982 when America permitted the Israelis to invade Lebanon and the American Sixth Fleet helped them in that. This bombardment began and many were killed and injured and others were terrorized and displaced."

The third aspect that deeply influenced bin Laden's thinking was the 1979 Soviet invasion of Afghanistan. The invasion profoundly disturbed him;

APRIL
1975
Lebanon descends into a brutal 15-year-long civil war

USS *New Jersey* firing her 16-inch guns at targets inside Lebanon in 1984, during that country's civil war. Two decades later, bin Laden continued to cite this conflict as the most profound influence on his beliefs and actions. (David Buell/US Navy)

motivated by the perceived injustices committed against his fellow Muslims, as well as by the opportunity to distinguish himself, he threw himself into supporting the Afghan mujahideen cause. With Saudi endorsement and support from various other sources, he helped to recruit thousands of Muslim fighters for the resistance and to raise hundreds of millions of dollars. Bin Laden eventually went into Afghanistan to lend support in person to the cause. It was in this way – at the dawning of the information age – that he came to be identified as a key public face of the jihadist movement, achieving something akin to celebrity status. His opposition to "foreign" military interventions in Muslim nations continued after Afghanistan. He condemned the deployment of US-led coalition forces to his home nation of Saudi Arabia in 1990 prior to the Gulf War, the 1991 liberation and occupation of Kuwait, and the 1992–94 US intervention in Somalia.

Bin Laden repeatedly referred back to – and thus defined his personal and political identity through – these three fundamental influences. Together with many other similar geo-political influences across the closing decades of the 20th century, they gave him a clear motive and purpose, and produced a person the world came to fear.

DECEMBER
1979
Soviet forces invade Afghanistan

A jihadist education

While bin Laden's interest in radicalism may have been strong, influences during both his formal and informal education were to play a significant part in spurring him to express these in action. His schooling began in Saudi Arabia, alongside many other affluent Muslim children, in Saudi Arabia's secular al-Thager Model School. He then studied economics and business administration at King Abdulaziz University in Jeddah, although he failed to graduate. However, it was his informal education that had the greatest impact. Just as three significant emotional events provided much of his motivation to act, three equally significant lessons during his informal education directly shaped his methods and objectives as a jihadist.

The Muslim Brotherhood

Bin Laden was introduced to the teachings of the Egyptian Islamist radical Sayyid Qutb (1906–66) while still a young, wealthy college student. Qutb was a leading member of the Egyptian Muslim Brotherhood during the 1950s and early 1960s, until his execution in 1966 for plotting the assassination of President Nasser. By the time of the outbreak of the Lebanese Civil War bin Laden was a fully committed member of the Muslim Brotherhood, espousing the Prophet Mohammed's earliest teachings. Bin Laden believed that, firstly, a jihad against all unbelievers was a holy obligation and, secondly, that worldwide revolution to safeguard the mission of spreading Islam was necessary to destroy corrupt societies and convert the world. The young bin Laden received extensive mentorship and attention from the most persuasive teachers of the Brotherhood. Where his secular education left off, militant jihadist extremism stepped in.

The lessons of Beirut and Afghanistan

With such a deep personal attachment to Beirut, bin Laden closely followed the tragic events unfolding in Lebanon from 1975 onward. What he saw convinced him that the United States, Israel and the Western world were intent on implementing a systematic plan to wipe out the Arabs, Islam and nearly 1,500 years of Muslim culture. In June 1982 Israel Defense Forces (IDF) troops invaded southern Lebanon, with the aim of expelling Palestine Liberation Organization (PLO) forces, ending Syrian control over Lebanon and installing a pro-Israeli government.

The Soviet occupation of Afghanistan is often characterized as the making of bin Laden. The deep anger he felt over these events motivated his militant actions. (RIA Novosti/ CC-BY-SA-3.0)

The suicide bombing of the US Embassy in Beirut on April 18, 1983 killed 63 people. The following year, after the hugely destructive truck bombings of US and French barracks in Beirut, multinational forces began withdrawing from Lebanon. Osama bin Laden took this as a lesson and an example of what could be effected through terrorism. (US Army)

In September of that year, US President Ronald Reagan deployed US Marines to a multinational force to restore the Lebanese government.

Bin Laden's overshadowing "lesson of Beirut" was born out of the events of 1983. In April, 63 people were killed when a suicide bomber detonated a van full of explosives outside the US embassy in the city. On October 23, two truck bombs – assembled by Imad Mughniyah, an Iranian-trained Hezbollah member – destroyed the US Marine and French Army barracks in Beirut, killing hundreds. Shortly after this attack, US and multinational forces were compelled to withdraw from Beirut; the events also pressured Israeli forces to follow suit. Bin Laden celebrated this as a huge victory over powerful nations and was ominously impressed by this example – so much so that he sent his own bomb makers to Mughniyah in Lebanon for training in the 1990s. Bin Laden concluded that the world's most powerful nations could only be defeated this way, a view he asserted in a 2004 speech broadcast by Al Jazeera:

> All that we have mentioned has made it easy for us to provoke and bait this administration. All that we have to do is to send two mujahideen to the furthest point east to raise a piece of cloth on which is written al-Qaeda, in order to make the generals race there to cause America to suffer human, economic, and political losses without their achieving for it anything of note other than some benefits for their private companies.

In the years following his first contact with the Afghan resistance against the Soviets in 1979 (while based in Pakistan), bin Laden came to realize that he could use his family's worldwide business connections to solicit and raise vast amounts of money from wealthy Muslims, particularly those in the Middle East.

In the mid-1980s bin Laden, the Palestinian Abdullah Yusuf Azzam (bin Laden's mentor), and Abdullah Anas (Azzam's son-in-law) created an organization called Maktab al-Khidamat (MAK), known in English as "the Services Office" (and also known as "al-Kifah"); this played a key role in the private funding network that fought against Russian control. Through this organization bin Laden supported several Afghan resistance groups, recruited volunteers worldwide, sponsored thousands of Muslim fighters, and funded multiple training camps for them. Within the space of several years he controlled a multi-million dollar operation, built upon an extensive global network of multi-tiered financial resources and a following of many thousands of jihadist supporters. In 1986 bin Laden used his resources to establish a training camp system called al-Masadah, or "the Lion's Den"; its mission was to provide fighters and resources from Persian Gulf states for the Afghan resistance. This, however, was not enough for bin Laden. When he eventually entered combat in person in Afghanistan some years later, it was with the intent of validating his status as a "jihadist warrior."

OCTOBER 23, 1983

299 US and French service personnel die in the Beirut barracks bombings

When the last Soviet forces withdrew from Afghanistan in 1989, ending a bloody and prolonged war of attrition, bin Laden again celebrated a "defeat of the infidel superpowers," just as he had done in Beirut. However, the prevailing lesson of the Soviet–Afghan War became clearer to him some time later, with the 1991 collapse and disintegration of the Soviet Union. Bin Laden reflected that the superpowers could also be provoked into a lengthy war of attrition, resulting in massive financial burdens, shifts in perception, political fragmentation, and eventually self-destruction. He showed the influence of these ideas in a speech broadcast by Al Jazeera in 2004:

> having experience in using guerrilla warfare and the war of attrition to fight tyrannical superpowers, we, alongside the mujahideen, bled Russia for 10 years, until it went bankrupt and was forced to withdraw in defeat. All Praise is due to Allah. So we are continuing this policy in bleeding America to the point of bankruptcy.

A mujahid ("one who struggles for Islam") in Afghanistan demonstrates how to fire a Soviet-built SA-7 hand-held surface-to-air missile. (DoD)

Afghans in the city of Peshawar showing off the canopy of a downed Soviet jet in 1984. (Erwin Lux/ CC-BY-SA-3.0)

Each of these aspects of Osama bin Laden's "jihadist education" led him to formulate his plan for a worldwide revolution "to destroy corrupt societies and bring the world to Islam," and a global strategy of violent terrorist attacks to provoke the superpowers into their own self-destruction. With his Muslim Brotherhood mentors, bin Laden began advocating a global jihad beyond the war in Afghanistan. To fulfil this vision, he needed a base organization to both direct and inspire its followers; its name would be al-Qaeda.

al-Qaeda – "the Base"

Sometime between mid-1988 and 1989, as Soviet forces began to withdraw from Afghanistan, bin Laden co-founded al-Qaeda ("the Base") with his teacher and mentor, the Palestinian Abdullah Yusuf Azzam; other influential figures in the early organization included. Mohammed Atef and Abu Ubaidah al-Banshiri. Operating out of Afghanistan and Peshawar, Pakistan (a city close to the border between the two countries), the organization was founded to continue the jihadist struggle in other parts of the world, not just Afghanistan. The existence of the organization was kept a closely guarded secret. Members had to promise to follow the instructions of their leaders without question and behave impeccably. As the last Soviet forces withdrew from Afghanistan in 1989, leaving behind over a million dead Afghans, bin Laden celebrated what he termed the "defeat of infidel super-powers."

FEBRUARY 15, 1989

Soviet forces complete their withdrawal from Afghanistan

Gradually, bin Laden rose to the top of this new organization, a move facilitated by the assassination of Abdullah Yusuf Azzam on November 24, 1989 in a car bomb attack in Peshawar. Bin Laden found himself perfectly situated to re-direct the resources of the extensive network he had helped build, moving its focus away from a regional conflict to a global campaign under his control. He methodically diverted all of its assets, its financial supporters, the religious guidance it offered, and its capacity for media operations, as well as many of its followers, from Afghan resistance into waging a worldwide jihad based upon violence and terrorism.

Bin Laden now returned to Saudi Arabia. US forces had deployed there from August 1990 in preparation for operations *Desert Shield* and *Desert Storm* against Iraq. Bin Laden was outraged by the presence of infidel troops so near to the Mecca and Medina holy sites and expressed open dissent. As a result, he was expelled from Saudi Arabia, and relocated with his followers (and assets of up to $250 million) to Sudan. He continued to maintain offices and guesthouses in Pakistan, and multiple training camps in Afghanistan and Sudan, signaling the rise of al-Qaeda into a terrorist network operating on a global scale.

FEBRUARY 1998

Bin Laden's fatwa states "Muslims should kill Americans including civilians"

During the early 1990s bin Laden initiated interaction with Hezbollah and Iran to take part in a global war against the US. He also funded jihadists in Algeria and Egypt, and (as already noted) sent several al-Qaeda operatives to Lebanon for explosives training from Hezbollah terrorist Imad Mughniyah. Throughout the mid-1990s he established and funded extensive terrorist training facilities in Sudan and Yemen near the Saudi border.

Following the failure of Operation *Gothic Serpent* (the 1993 US special operations intervention in Somalia aimed at capturing warlord Mohamed Farrah Aidid), bin Laden again celebrated what he saw as "victory over infidel superpowers." He mocked Americans as "paper tigers" after President Clinton ordered the withdrawal of American forces from the country.

However, bin Laden's growing prominence put him at risk. In February 1994 he suffered an assassination attempt – most likely a fire-fight between rival terrorists – at home in Sudan. Several people were killed in the attack. As a result, bin Laden intensified his personal protection forces and upgraded all of his security practices.

In May 1996 following international pressure, Sudan expelled bin Laden,

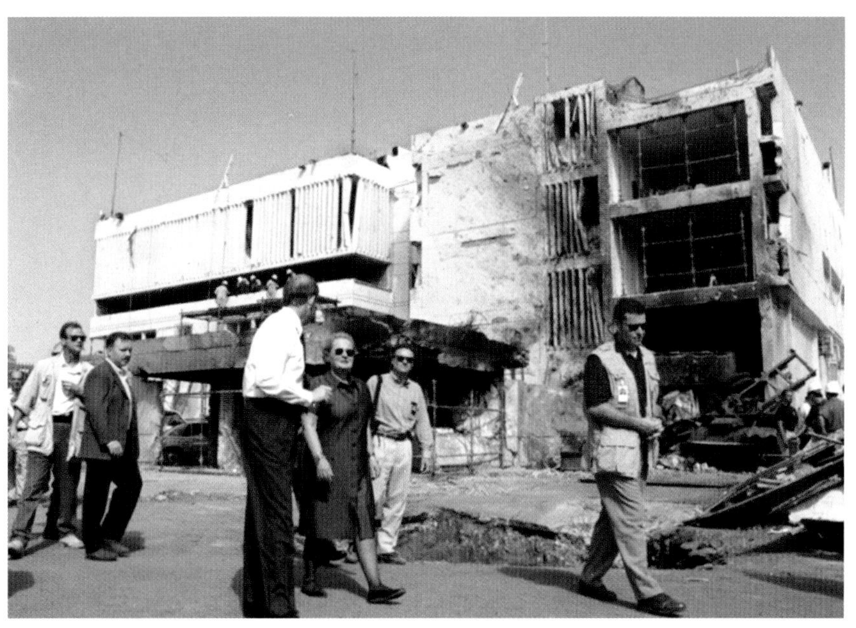

US Secretary of State Madeleine Albright walks past the bombed US embassy in Dar es Salaam, Tanzania on August 18, 1998. This attack, together with the simultaneous suicide truck bombing of the US Embassy in Nairobi, Kenya, signaled a dramatic escalation in the threat posed by al-Qaeda to the international community, and US citizens and service personnel in particular. (Alexander Joe/AFP/Getty Images)

THE GROWTH OF TERROR: AL-QAEDA, 1990–2001

December 29, 1992 The Yemen hotel bombings – al-Qaeda's first (known) terrorist attacks – fail to kill US and UN military personnel in Aden who are deploying to Somalia. Bin Laden claims responsibility with Mohammed Khan.

February 26, 1993 The World Trade Center truck bomb is detonated by Ramzi Yousef (nephew of 9/11 planner Khalid Sheikh Mohammed) killing six, and wounding hundreds. Bin Laden is named as a co-conspirator.

October 1993 Bin Laden's Afghanistan-trained "Arab holy warriors" and Somali Muslims ambush and kill 18 US servicemen supporting humanitarian missions in Mogadishu, Somalia.

February 7, 1995 Ramzi Yousef, the World Trade Center truck bomber, is captured in Pakistan and extradited to the US. There is evidence of financial and other support reaching Yousef from bin Laden.

February–December 1995 Bin laden funds a series of attacks with Ayman al-Zawahiri, including a suicide bombing at the Egyptian Embassy in Pakistan and failed attempts to kill the Egyptian president Hosni Mubarak.

November 13, 1995 Five Americans and two Indians are killed by a truck bomb at the US-operated Saudi National Guard training center in Riyadh, Saudi Arabia.

June 25, 1996 The Khobar Towers housing complex is bombed near Dhahran, Saudi Arabia. 19 American soldiers are killed and 500 people are wounded. Bin Laden and al-Qaeda are implicated.

February 1997 Bin Laden orders the militarization of the East African cell of al-Qaeda, which will lead to the Kenya and Tanzania embassy bombings in August 1998.

November 17, 1997 Bin Laden funds terrorist attacks in Luxor, Egypt.

August 7, 1998 al-Qaeda operatives bomb the US embassies in Nairobi, Kenya and Dar es Salaam, Tanzania killing 224 people and wounding several thousand.

January 3, 2000 al-Qaeda operatives abort an attack on the USS *The Sullivans* when the weight of explosives sinks their boat. The sunken explosives are later recovered for use in the attack against the USS *Cole*.

October 12, 2000 The USS *Cole* is damaged in an al-Qaeda suicide boat attack in Aden, Yemen, killing 17 sailors and wounding 39.

January–December 2000 Several al-Qaeda plots fail, including a planned bomb attack on a hotel in Amman, Jordan; an attack on Mount Nebo, Jordan; an attack at a site on the River Jordan; and a bomb attack at Los Angeles International Airport.

May 29, 2001 Four al-Qaeda supporters are convicted for the 1998 US embassy bombings in Africa.

May–September 2001 Multiple teams of al-Qaeda terrorists assemble and train at various US locations in preparation for the simultaneous hijacking attempts of September 11.

September 11, 2001 The 9/11 terrorist attacks take place, with devastating results.

An aerial view of the World Trade Center site, bounded by Vesey, Church, and Liberty streets and Route 9A, following the September 11, 2001 attack. This photograph was taken by Eric J. Tilford, US Navy, on September 17. (Library of Congress)

and he returned to Afghanistan with his family and followers, where he was hosted by Taliban rulers. In 1997 attacks by the Afghan Northern Alliance forced him to abandon his Najim Jihad compound and move south to Tarnak Farms near Kandahar. He continued to build his relationship with the Taliban by sending several hundred fighters to aid their cause.

Bin Laden's anti-US rhetoric became increasingly virulent in this period. From his bases in Afghanistan, he exploited his media contacts and skills to threaten a jihad or "holy war" against the US and its allies if Washington did not remove troops from the Gulf region. In February 1998 he published a joint fatwa (or religious ruling) with Ayman al-Zawahiri (Egyptian founder of Islamic Jihad, and later leader of al-Qaeda following bin Laden's death) stating that "Muslims should kill Americans including civilians – anywhere in the world." Throughout this period, bin Laden's rhetoric was backed up by ever-increasing bloodshed caused by his al-Qaeda operatives.

al-Qaeda's long-term strategic plan

In 2005 intelligence work brought al-Qaeda's 20-year strategic plan to light. Worthy of note are five key stages within this (summarized below) that directly reflect bin Laden's motives and methods.

1. Provoke the United States and the West into invading a Muslim country [e.g. Afghanistan, or Iraq] by staging a massive attack or string of attacks on US soil resulting in high numbers of civilian casualties.
2. Incite local resistance to occupying forces.

The corner of Greenwich and Barclay, facing east, near the destroyed World Trade Center. (Library of Congress)

THE THREAT OF MASS DESTRUCTION: AL-QAEDA, 2001–11

January–December 1992 Bin Laden begins efforts to obtain chemical and nuclear weapon components.

May 29, 1998 Bin Laden issues a statement entitled "The Nuclear Bomb of Islam" propounding the idea that "it is the duty of all Muslims to prepare as much force as possible to terrorize the enemies of God."

August 12, 1998 President Clinton is presented evidence indicating that bin Laden is seeking to develop weapons of mass destruction for use against the United States.

February 2000 The al-Qaeda defector Jamal Ahmed al-Fadl testifies that Osama Bin Laden is trying to buy uranium on the black market for $1.5 million in order to develop nuclear weapons.

October 11, 2001 Two "nuclear suitcases" are reported to have reached al-Qaeda operatives in the United States.

November 2001 A communication from bin Laden states nuclear weapons are available in Russia for $10 or $20 million; al-Qaeda spiritual leader Mullah Mohammed Omar claims that the nuclear destruction of the United States is under way.

March 2, 2003 Khalid Sheikh Mohammed reveals bin Laden's plan to create a "nuclear hell-storm" by constructing and detonating dirty nukes in the US.

January–December 2003 Osama bin Laden allegedly pays over $60 million for the expertise of Pakistani nuclear engineers and specialists, as well as former Soviet and Chinese nuclear scientists and technicians. Bin Laden also allegedly purchases 12kg of uranium for over $75 million – though no weapon materializes.

3. Expand the conflict to neighboring countries, and engage the US and its allies in a long war of attrition.
4. Convert al-Qaeda into an ideology and set of operating principles that can be loosely franchised in other countries without requiring direct command and control. Via these franchises, incite attacks against the US and allied countries until they withdraw from conflict.
5. Following the collapse of the US economy around the year 2020 (brought about by the strain of multiple engagements), the worldwide economic system (which is dependent on the US) will also collapse, leading to global political instability. This in turn brings about a global jihad led by al-Qaeda and a Wahhabi caliphate will then be installed across the world following the collapse of the US and other Western countries.

(Abdel Bari Atwan, 2006, p. 221)

His intent was to wage a war of attrition against the United States culminating in its economic and political collapse, which in turn would trigger a global jihad. With this conflict projected to last much longer than the decade-long Soviet–Afghan War – up to 20 or more years – bin Laden often inferred that he did not expect to live to see its final stages. Moreover, bin Laden began to seek ways to inflict the maximum amount of damage and destruction on his sworn enemies, including the use of nuclear weapons.

INITIAL STRATEGY

A ten-year manhunt

US intelligence knew from the outset that Osama bin Laden was ultimately responsible for the terrorist attacks of September 11, 2001 (or "9/11," to use the shortened form); known al-Qaeda operatives were detected on passenger lists of the doomed aircraft. The day following the attacks, US President George W. Bush told the American public, "The most important thing is for us to find Osama bin Laden… It is our number one priority and we will not rest until we find him." Within a month, the US launched Operation *Enduring Freedom* in Afghanistan. The invasion of the country ostensibly sought to destroy al-Qaeda and overthrow the ruling Taliban, which was harboring its supporters. However, the initial, critical goal of the operation was the same as that of Operation *Neptune Spear* in 2011: to hunt down Osama bin Laden. Indeed, since the mid-1990s an intensive intelligence effort had been underway to locate the leader of al-Qaeda.

By December 2001, bin Laden had been tracked down to the remote White Mountains (Safed Koh) in eastern Afghanistan. US and allied forces conducted a major combined-arms offensive and attempted to isolate the al-Qaeda stronghold known as Tora Bora. Hundreds of al-Qaeda and Taliban fighters were killed or captured, but inexplicably, bin Laden successfully eluded capture in the battle's aftermath.

In the ten years following 9/11, the location of Osama bin Laden was a closely guarded secret. The worldwide news media continued to speculate on his whereabouts, including projections about his death, his failing health and his plotting of "the next 9/11." During this period bin Laden periodically released video and audio recordings to the media, always referring to current events as time markers and asserting that he was well and leading al-Qaeda and the jihad against America. Bin Laden had managed to disappear, but he had not given up his fight. His enemies, likewise, did not give up their pursuit.

SEPTEMBER 12, 2001

George W. Bush states, "The most important thing is for us to find Osama bin Laden"

OUT FROM THE SHADOWS: SEEKING BIN LADEN, 1995–2000

October 21, 1995 US President Bill Clinton launches an interagency effort to track bin Laden's financial transactions and resources.

January 1996 The CIA and FBI establish the Bin Laden Issue Station (codenamed Alec Station) to track down bin Laden and his associates in the al-Qaeda network.

April 1996 President Clinton signs a top-secret order authorizing the CIA to use any and all means to destroy bin Laden's network.

July 1997 The CIA reportedly employs mercenary forces to find, abduct or kill bin Laden in Afghanistan.

1998 The chief of Alec Station arranges an operation to kill or capture Osama bin Laden; however, it is vetoed by the Riyadh CIA station chief, stating: "The Americans should trust the Saudis to take care of bin Laden."

July–August 1998 US intelligence intercepts of mobile phone conversations between bin Laden lieutenants pinpoint their locations, reveal their intentions, and implicate them in the US embassy bombings.

August 1998 President Clinton signs an authorization for the CIA to capture bin Laden using force. A follow-up memo authorizes the assassination of up to ten other al-Qaeda leaders, as well as the shooting down of any private aircraft containing bin Laden.

August 20, 1998 Operation *Infinite Reach* (an attempt to assassinate bin Laden) takes place. Using intelligence from mobile phone intercepts, the US Navy launches 66 Tomahawk cruise missiles at suspected al-Qaeda training camps in Khost, Afghanistan, as well as a plant in Sudan suspected of producing chemical weapons for bin Laden. Although 30 people are reportedly killed, bin Laden survives. From now on, he ceases to communicate using phones.

December 24, 1998 President Clinton authorizes the assassination of bin Laden by a group of CIA "tribal assets" in Afghanistan who are monitoring bin Laden. The authorization is not communicated within the CIA – not even to Michael Scheuer, head of Alec Station.

February 1999 President Clinton allows the CIA to use the Northern Alliance in an operation to assassinate Osama bin Laden. The president himself deletes the wording authorizing a CIA operation to kill bin Laden.

June, 7 1999 Bin Laden appears for the first time on the FBI's Ten Most Wanted Fugitives list.

October 12, 1999 A joint US–Pakistani operation to capture bin Laden is aborted when General Pervez Musharraf overthrows elected Prime Minister Nawaz Sharif.

March 2000 An assassination attempt takes place by CIA-hired mercenaries using RPGs to ambush bin Laden's convoy in the Afghanistan mountains. Bin Laden's vehicle is not hit.

DECEMBER 12–17, 2001

US forces attack the Tora Bora cave complex in Afghanistan

The US rapidly accumulated a steady flow of "detainees" captured in Afghanistan. Supported by its allies, it also conducted a worldwide roundup of all persons ever known to have associated with bin Laden or al-Qaeda. By early 2002, the CIA and US military had begun to process and interrogate captured al-Qaeda suspects at a detention centre in Guantanamo Bay, Cuba and other secret facilities or "black sites" outside of the US. The CIA carefully compiled data on all suspected leaders, couriers, moneymen and subordinates. Although the general objective was to defeat and destroy al-Qaeda and associated terrorists, finding bin Laden was the ultimate goal.

In 1998 bin Laden's use of the telephone drew US missile strikes on his Sudan and Afghanistan bases. As a result, he stopped using telephones from that point onwards, and made himself very hard to find. He carefully

Tora Bora, known locally as Spion Ghar, is a cave complex situated in the White Mountains (Safed Koh) in eastern Afghanistan. It had been used as a base for mujahideen fighters since the 1980s. (SSgt Russell Lee Klika/US Army)

concealed his movements and locations from everyone, including his own subordinates. He only communicated with his al-Qaeda followers, the organization's leadership and the media through trusted and experienced couriers. Thus, tracking him with electronic surveillance was going to prove difficult for the US and its allies. His seekers were left with few "human intelligence" methods to find him. It may never be revealed if any informants or undercover operatives were involved in keeping track of his whereabouts, but it would appear likely that, to some degree, this was the case. Reportedly, the approach that ultimately proved successful was the identification and location of his couriers.

Key leads – mistaking the courier

The first crucial "courier lead" in the hunt for Osama bin Laden did not gain due notice at first. In early 2002, only a few months into Operation *Enduring Freedom,* the CIA collected intelligence on a man named Ibrahim Saeed Ahmed, who was an al-Qaeda operative and possible bin Laden associate. This information would prove critical but was not yet understood; as a result, the intelligence was filed away and it did not resurface until 2010.

Later in 2002, the CIA began to gather uncorroborated data on the nom de guerre, or al-Qaeda operative name, of Abu Ahmed al-Kuwaiti. This person was initially only referred to by this operative name; further confusion was also added by translating this as Sheikh Abu Ahmed from Kuwait, together with spelling variations. He was suspected of being a mid-level al-Qaeda operative who facilitated the movements of and organized safe havens for senior al-Qaeda members and their families.

JANUARY 11, 2002

First 20 detainees arrive at Guantanamo Bay, Cuba

BIN LADEN'S ROUTE TO ABBOTTABAD, 2001–05

Where did the world's most wanted man hide for nearly ten years? Information gathered after Operation *Neptune Spear* from his surviving spouses and various documents have pinpointed his movements and hiding places after the October 2001 US and UK invasions of Afghanistan.

September 12, 2001 US President George W. Bush states, "The most important thing is for us to find Osama bin Laden."

October 7, 2001 US and coalition forces launch Operation *Enduring Freedom* to attack Taliban and al-Qaeda forces in Afghanistan.

November 27, 2001 Bin Laden is detected in the Tora Bora area with al-Qaeda supporters. American and British special forces plan a major assault with Afghan allies and extensive US air support.

December 12–17, 2001 At Tora Bora, US/NATO and Afghan Northern Alliance fighters defeat some Taliban and al-Qaeda forces, but bin Laden leaves the region.

December 27, 2001 Afghan officials report bin Laden to be amongst al-Qaeda sympathizers operating out of Pakistan.

April 2002 Bin Laden is re-united with his wives – for the first time since the 9/11 attacks – in Peshawar, the border city of 3.5 million inhabitants.

September 2002 Bin Laden and his family relocate from Peshawar to the Shangla district in the Swat valley in rural northwest Pakistan for about nine months (away from the "tribal belt" areas, where the US focus is concentrated).

March 20, 2003 The US and coalition forces invade Iraq.

May 2003 Bin Laden and his family relocate from northwest Pakistan to the village of Chak Shah Mohammad in the Haripur district, 20 miles south of Abbottabad, Pakistan. They live in a rented house for over two years.

2004 Bin Laden's courier Abu Ahmed al-Kuwaiti oversees construction of a three-story compound in a residential area 2.5 miles (4km) northeast of Abbottabad.

June 2005 Bin Laden begins to occupy the compound with two wives, six children and four grandchildren. The courier al-Kuwaiti and his younger brother Abrar also move in with their wives. They are later joined by one of bin Laden's sons, Khalid.

October 2005 CIA increases the placement of case officers on the ground in Pakistan and Afghanistan, but also closes the unit code-named Alec Station tasked with hunting down Osama bin Laden and his top lieutenants. It was "changing its focus to regional trends instead of specific individuals."

In 2002, a detainee at Guantanamo, Mohamedou Ould Salahi, gave credible assertions that he had witnessed a mid-level al-Qaeda operative named Abu Ahmed al-Kuwaiti die of wounds inflicted in the December 2001 battle of Tora Bora. This operative, according to Salahi, had facilitated the movement of and finding safe havens for senior al-Qaeda members and families. The courier-lead to "al-Kuwaiti" appeared to have turned cold, literally.

However, the lead was later resurrected with information from Mohammed Mana Ahmed al-Qahtani (or al-Kahtani). He was a Saudi citizen who had been detained at Guantanamo Bay as an enemy combatant since June 2002. Al-Qahtani had tried to enter the USA in 2001, ostensibly to take part in the 9/11 attacks as the twentieth hijacker. However, he was refused entry, and was later captured in Afghanistan after the 2001 Tora Bora battle. Interrogations of al-Qahtani between November 2002 and January 2003 indicated that the courier named Abu Ahmed al-Kuwaiti was not dead, but operating as part of the inner circle of al-Qaeda. Still, nothing further could be ascertained about the whereabouts or true identity of this man, and after

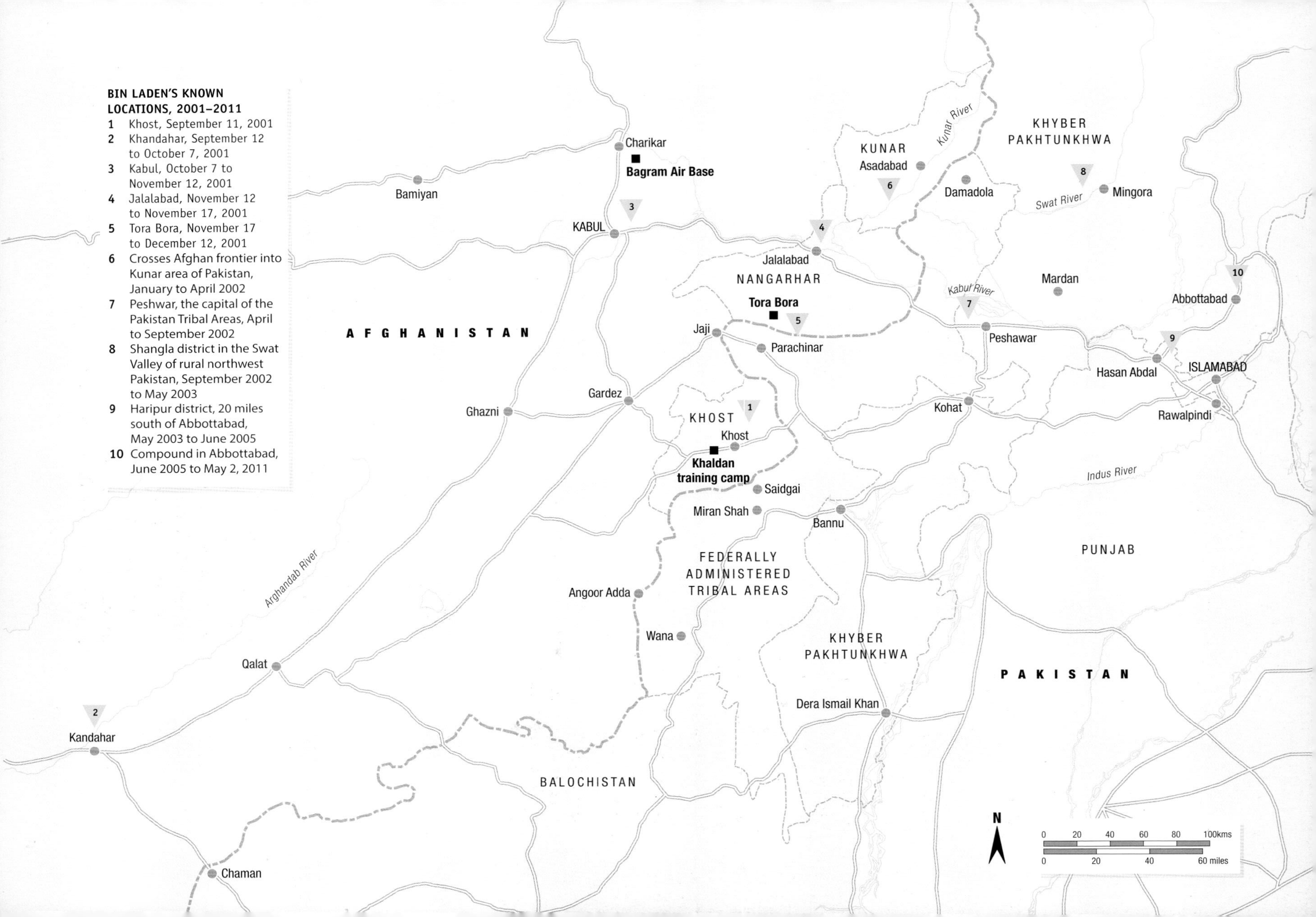

BIN LADEN'S KNOWN LOCATIONS, 2001–2011
1 Khost, September 11, 2001
2 Khandahar, September 12 to October 7, 2001
3 Kabul, October 7 to November 12, 2001
4 Jalalabad, November 12 to November 17, 2001
5 Tora Bora, November 17 to December 12, 2001
6 Crosses Afghan frontier into Kunar area of Pakistan, January to April 2002
7 Peshwar, the capital of the Pakistan Tribal Areas, April to September 2002
8 Shangla district in the Swat Valley of rural northwest Pakistan, September 2002 to May 2003
9 Haripur district, 20 miles south of Abbottabad, May 2003 to June 2005
10 Compound in Abbottabad, June 2005 to May 2, 2011
AFGHANISTAN
PAKISTAN
KHYBER PAKHTUNKHWA
KUNAR
NANGARHAR
KHOST
FEDERALLY ADMINISTERED TRIBAL AREAS
PUNJAB
BALOCHISTAN
Charikar
Bagram Air Base
Bamiyan
KABUL
Ghazni
Gardez
Jaji
Tora Bora
Parachinar
Jalalabad
Asadabad
Damadola
Mingora
Mardan
Peshawar
Abbottabad
Hasan Abdal
ISLAMABAD
Rawalpindi
Kohat
Khost
Khaldan training camp
Saidgai
Miran Shah
Bannu
Angoor Adda
Wana
Dera Ismail Khan
Qalat
Kandahar
Chaman
Kunar River
Swat River
Kabul River
Indus River
Arghandab River
N
0 20 40 60 80 100kms
0 20 40 60 miles

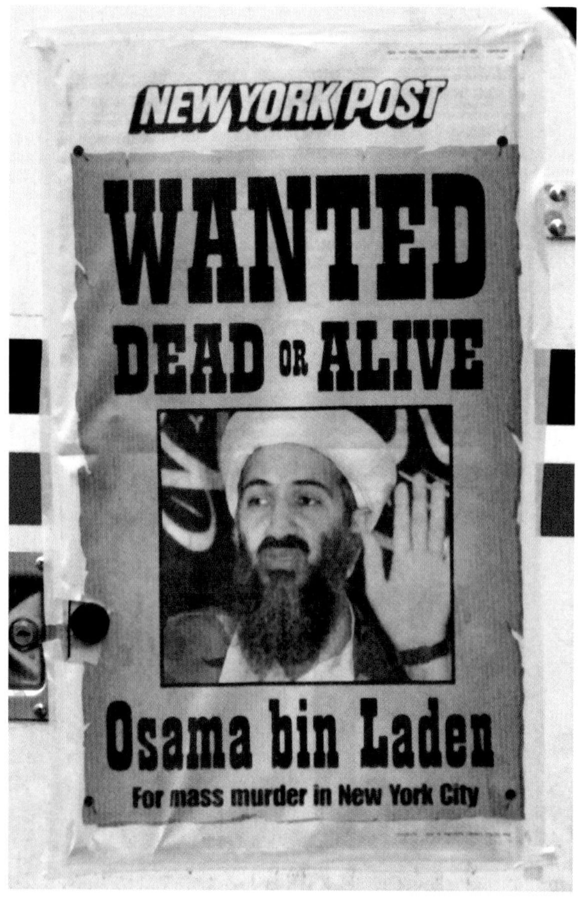

"WANTED DEAD OR ALIVE" – A *New York Post* poster from September 19, 2001. (Art Seitz/Gamma-Rapho via Getty Images)

two years the hunt for bin Laden through his courier had again stalled.

On February 1, 2003 the al-Qaeda operational chief and the alleged architect of the 9/11 attacks, Khalid Sheik Mohammed, was captured in the Pakistani city of Karachi. During interrogation between October and December 2004, he denied knowing any courier named al-Kuwaiti. Then, shortly afterwards, he admitted that he did know him. However, he said al-Kuwaiti "was not active in al-Qaeda."

None of this was deemed of major significance until 2005, when al-Qaeda courier and operative Hassan Ghul (real name, Mustafa Hajji Muhammad Khan), who had been captured in northern Iraq in January of the previous year, revealed that al-Kuwaiti was close to bin Laden and Khalid Sheikh Mohammed, as well as al-Qaeda operational chief Abu Faraj al-Libi. He also noted that al-Kuwaiti had not been seen in some time. All of this raised suspicion that al-Kuwaiti could be close to bin Laden. Hassan Ghul also revealed in 2005 that Abu Ahmed al-Kuwaiti was a nom de guerre, and that al-Kuwaiti was "crucial to al-Qaeda."

On May 2, 2005 Abu Faraj al-Libi (who was the successor to Khalid Sheikh Mohammed) was captured in the northern Pakistani city of Mardan. During interrogation in 2006, he denied knowing anyone named al-Kuwaiti. He claimed bin Laden's courier was called Maulawi Abd al-Khaliq Jan – a fake name. With both Khalid Sheikh Mohammed and Abu Faraj al-Libi attempting to play down his importance, the inference was that al-Kuwaiti might indeed be part of bin Laden's inner circle.

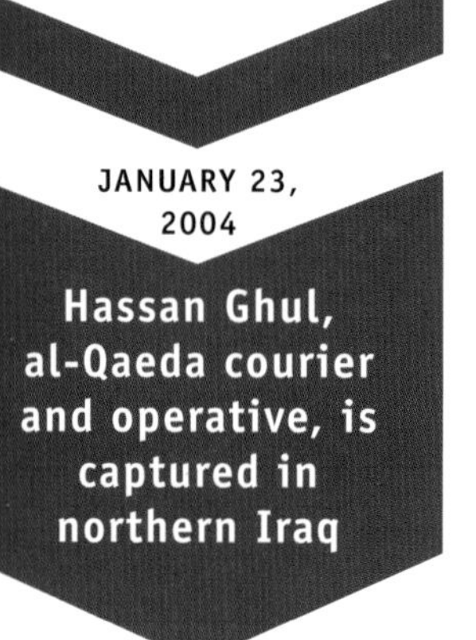

JANUARY 23, 2004
Hassan Ghul, al-Qaeda courier and operative, is captured in northern Iraq

Abu Ahmed al-Kuwaiti remained a mystery man until 2007, when the CIA discovered his real name via his family origins in Kuwait. By 2008 his telephone and emails between Kuwait and Pakistan were being intercepted, which eventually led to his identity being revealed. Abu Ahmed al-Kuwaiti was Ibrahim Saeed Ahmed. He also used the aliases Mohammed Arshad, Ibrahim Saeed Ahmed and Arshad Khan. In addition, by late 2010 the Pakistani Inter-Services Intelligence agency (ISI) had been cooperating to provide the CIA with al-Kuwaiti's cell phone number as last detected in Abbottabad, allowing months of his phone usage in Pakistan to be tracked.

In August 2010, after extensive phone tracking, Abu Ahmed al-Kuwaiti was followed as he drove from Peshawar to Abbottabad and then entered an imposing, fort-like compound there. The nature of the Abbottabad compound was an immediate indication that the CIA had found a "high value target,"

KEY LEADS IN THE MANHUNT

2001–2002: Interrogation of Mohamedou Ould Salahi revealed that "Abu Ahmed al-Kuwaiti" was a mid-level al-Qaeda courier and operative who also handled movements and safe havens for senior al-Qaeda members and their families. But reports suggest he died in December 2001 from wounds after the Tora Bora battle.

2002–2003: Interrogations of Mohammed Mana Ahmed al-Qahtani indicate "Abu Ahmed al-Kuwaiti" is alive and part of the inner circle of al-Qaeda

2003–2004: Khalid Sheikh Mohammed, al-Qaeda operations chief and alleged 9/11 architect, is captured. In 2004 interrogations he denied knowing a courier named al-Kuwaiti, but later admitted it, although he claimed "al-Kuwaiti is not active in al-Qaeda."

2004–2005: Interrogation of Hassan Ghul, al-Qaeda operative and courier, reveals bin Laden courier Abu Ahmed al-Kuwaiti is close to bin Laden, Khalid Sheikh Mohammed, and Abu Faraj al-Libi.

2005–2006: Abu Faraj al-Libi, al-Qaeda operations chief, is captured in the north of Pakistan. Interrogations in 2006 result in a denial that he knows al-Kuwaiti.

Khalid Sheikh Mohammed.

2007–2008: The CIA identifies the family name of Abu Ahmed al-Kuwaiti (a.k.a. Sheikh Abu Ahmed, Arshad Khan Mohammed Arshad, and Ibraim Saeed Ahmed). The NSA is directed to intercept telephone calls and emails to Pakistan.

2009–2010: Abu Ahmed al-Kuwaiti is located in Pakistan and tracked to bin Laden's compound in Abbottabad.

possibly the world's most wanted man – Osama bin Laden. Abu Ahmed al-Kuwaiti was a perfect fit for the courier role. He was a Pakistani who was born in Kuwait, and he spoke both Arabic and native Pashto. He could communicate well with al-Qaeda Arabs as well as both urban and tribal Pakistanis. He was able to function openly in Pakistan using forged national identity cards, which he used to purchase and establish the bin Laden compound. Along with his brother (or cousin) Abrar al-Kuwaiti (a.k.a. Saeed Ahmed and Tareq Khan), he managed the residence where three families and up to 22 men, women, and children lived for over six years. Although Abu Ahmed al-Kuwaiti enabled bin Laden to live in Pakistan securely and in secrecy for so many years, he was also the man who led the Americans directly to him. Aside from all of this, it cannot be ruled out that an as-of-yet unidentified source discovered and/or reported bin Laden's presence. Furthermore, the existence of such a source might never be revealed.

To raid or not – a matter of decision

By mid-August 2010 the Pakistani ISI had provided the CIA with Abu Ahmed al-Kuwaiti's cell phone number, last detected in Abbottabad.

The SEALs had been operating in Afghanistan since the start of *Enduring Freedom*. Here, a special operator observes the destruction of an enemy munitions cache, in 2002. (PH1 Tim Turner/US Navy)

US intelligence operatives then found, positively identified and followed bin Laden's most-trusted courier to the compound in Abbottabad. Shortly thereafter (if not before) the CIA fully updated the US President, Barrack Obama, on bin Laden's probable discovery, and related intelligence. A decision process then began at operational, strategic and political levels.

It was portrayed as a difficult and protracted decision. CIA agents and operatives were elated that their years of effort might finally bear fruit. However, at strategic and political levels, caution and trepidation overruled any sense of urgency. Instead of an immediate scramble to assault the highly suspect compound, the reaction was apprehensive. Orders were sent back to confirm and verify the actual presence of Osama bin Laden. Operation *Neptune Spear* and the raid to kill Osama bin Laden would not be executed for another nine months. In effect, the only decision made immediately was to "not decide."

AUGUST 2010

Abu Ahmed al-Kuwaiti is followed to the bin Laden compound in Abbottabad

Had the suspected resident been anyone other than Osama bin Laden, every person in the compound could have been quickly arrested and detained within 48 hours. Hundreds of such special operations raids of opportunity had been conceived and successfully conducted (in Afghanistan and Pakistan) in far less time, and with far less reliable intelligence. US and Pakistani cooperation to identify and apprehend al-Qaeda terrorists in this region was fairly common, with tactical security increased by rapid reactions.

The lack of detail on all of the compound's inhabitants was of no serious consequence, at least not in Pakistan. In this region, the more usual and

BIN LADEN AND AL-QAEDA'S ACTIVITIES, 2003–11

May 13, 2003 In Saudi Arabia, al-Qaeda uses truck bombs against a western housing complex, killing 34 and wounding 194.

May 28, 2003 The Saudi authorities arrest 11 al-Qaeda suspects.

July 7, 2005 London bombs on bus and underground kill 52 people and the four suicide bombers, wounding over 700. Later, al-Qaeda claims responsibility.

January 29, 2010 From his Abbottabad compound, bin Laden reportedly releases audiotapes claiming al-Qaeda responsibility for various attempted Christmas Day 2009 terrorist attacks.

March 2010 Bin Laden reportedly releases more audiotapes, including one threatening retaliation if the US executes alleged 9/11 mastermind Khalid Sheikh Mohammed, who is being held at Guantanamo Bay.

October 2010 Bin Laden composes a 48-page memo to an al-Qaeda deputy on the state of the group, warning that their long-time sanctuary in Pakistan's Waziristan tribal areas was now too dangerous due to US drone strikes.

2011 Bin Laden continues to compose and send varied communications, while an estimated $30 million per year in assets are spent to sustain various selected al-Qaeda operations worldwide.

effective special operations procedure was to "raid first and ask questions later." Whether the mysterious compound was occupied by terrorists, drug lords or Pakistani officials, the identity of each inhabitant would become immediately obvious upon entering the compound by force. Also, al-Kuwaiti alone was a high value target and a confirmed al-Qaeda operative. He would be a prize catch for US or Pakistani intelligence, and the CIA or Pakistani ISI could have picked him up at any time. However, ultimately Abu Ahmed al-Kuwaiti was no ordinary al-Qaeda courier; this was no ordinary compound and the ultimate goal of Osama bin Laden was no ordinary target.

Regardless, caution won out. All options presented complications and risked politically charged consequences. The three most predominate complications were that (1) bin Laden's presence was not yet one hundred percent certain nor easily verifiable, (2) the suspected compound was deep inside the sovereign national borders of US ally Pakistan, and (3) the target itself was Osama bin Laden, the world's most notorious terrorist, the most wanted man in history and by far the most sensational high value target ever sought. Notification of his whereabouts would be the media event of the year, if not the decade.

By November 2010, the CIA had launched a concentrated intelligence collection effort with support from the US Department of Defense and multiple other agencies to verify bin Laden's presence. However, confirming

While advancing on a suspected location of al-Qaeda and Taliban forces in eastern Afghanistan in January 2002, a member of a US Navy SEAL team provides cover for his teammates. (US Navy)

that he was living inside this secure compound in Pakistan proved to be resource intensive, time consuming and ultimately unachievable.

Watching the Abbottabad compound

The huge, intensive, multi-platform surveillance operation had but one purpose: to collect intelligence on the Abbottabad compound in order to confirm or deny bin Laden's presence there. This all had to be conducted without compromising secrecy or driving him deeper into hiding. With that in mind, the CIA ruled out increased Pakistani involvement; CIA Chief Leon Panetta told Massimo Calabresi from *Time* on May 3, 2011, "It was decided that any effort to work with the Pakistanis could jeopardize the mission."

It is important to note that, although the Pakistani authorities did cooperate with the US before, during and after *Neptune Spear*, none were aware of bin Laden's presence and none were officially involved in the operation to kill him. Pakistan's Inter-Service Intelligence (ISI) had cooperated with the CIA in the region, and conducted combined counter-terrorism operations over many years. During this time, the ISI provided the CIA with limited local information without knowing Osama bin Laden was potentially involved. It is also evident that the CIA employed former Pakistani military and ISI operatives as private security contractors to obtain photos and detailed information on the Abbottabad compound and its occupants, without associating any of it with bin Laden. These efforts did not identify bin Laden, but proved to be accurate enough to corroborate many other intelligence and surveillance efforts and, later, aided planning for the raid.

FEBRUARY
2011
CIA reports "a sound intelligence basis" for action to pursue bin Laden

By the end of November 2010, the data collected had confirmed that bin Laden's courier Abu Ahmed al-Kuwaiti, his brother (or cousin) Abrar (Saeed Ahmed) and their families were living at and maintaining the Abbottabad compound. This was a starting point. CIA operatives (reportedly with the assistance of Pakistani security contractors) occupied a rented house near the compound and began several months of continual observation. CIA teams employed state-of-the-art telephoto lenses, thermal and infrared imaging and high-tech audio equipment for eavesdropping, as well as relying on old-fashioned informants and agents. The National Security Agency (NSA) continued to intercept any relevant telephone exchanges. The US National Geospatial-Intelligence Agency (NGA) was also tasked with developing detailed imagery and recording daily patterns of life inside the compound. The NGA developed three-dimensional depictions for each of the buildings, recorded local traffic patterns and compiled data on the apparent height and gender of each compound inhabitant.

By December 2010, the surveillance mission had grown so much that the CIA had to secure authority from the US Congress to "reallocate tens of millions of dollars within assorted agency budgets" in order to continue to fund these ongoing surveillance operations. Despite this, all efforts to obtain images or audio recordings and identify bin Laden failed. In an attempt to identify occupants of the compound as children or relatives of bin Laden, the CIA employed Pakistani doctor Shakil Afridi in February 2011. Afridi conducted a vaccination program in the Abbottabad community and sought to obtain DNA samples from suspected bin Laden family members within the compound. The attempt failed when men in the compound denied access to Afridi and his assistants. Despite these failures, intelligence collection operations did rule out most other identity possibilities, and confirmed other conclusions.

The CIA reported afterwards that, "No US spy agency was ever able to capture a photograph of bin Laden at the compound before the raid or a recording of the voice of the mysterious male figure whose family occupied the structure's top two floors." The CIA also employed an independent team to study all the evidence collected in the effort. The conclusion was that "No other candidate fitted the bill as well as bin Laden did." The Abbottabad compound was custom-built to hide someone of significance very likely to be Osama bin Laden. By February 2011 the CIA had reported there was "a sound intelligence basis" for developing courses of action to pursue bin Laden at the Abbottabad compound.

From the summer of 2010 until May of 2011, what would eventually become Operation *Neptune Spear* hung in the balance of confirming the identity of a man who had spent a large fortune and his life's work to make himself invisible.

US Army Civil Affairs soldiers distribute leaflets announcing the bounty on Osama bin Laden's head in Mazar-e Sharif, Afghanistan, on December 18, 2001. (SSgt Cecilio Ricardo/US Navy)

Complicating factors

Bin Laden's compound was in Abbottabad, a city in the interior of Pakistan. He lived within a few hundred feet of a military base and the Pakistan Military Academy. The property sat within the jurisdiction of the actual military cantonment community. US options there were far more limited than in the more remote frontier or less regulated tribal regions where US and Pakistani operations had been ongoing for some time. The Pakistanis had tolerated, but not encouraged the US use of drone-launched missile strikes in Pakistan's Waziristan tribal areas. These strikes had killed a growing number of key al-Qaeda leaders (as well as Pakistan locals). Such a strike in a residential area would be extremely problematic.

Although Pakistan was a US ally in the region, as a sovereign nation there is no doubt that it would have insisted on controlling or conducting any potential special operations. As a nation with a certain number of jihadist sympathizers within its security establishment, Pakistan had an extremely limited ability to conduct highly sensitive operations without a high risk of security compromise.

By January of 2011 the CIA had fully briefed (the then) Vice-Admiral William H. McRaven, Commander of the US military's Joint Special Operations Command (JSOC) on the possibility of a special operations mission to get bin Laden. McRaven responded that employing a commando raid would be a fairly "straightforward" approach. He also addressed concerns over the risks associated with entering Pakistan and potentially provoking a response from the Pakistani military.

JOINT INTELLIGENCE EFFORTS

2008 Pakistan's ISI detachment in Abbottabad launches an investigation into Arshad Khan (Abu Ahmed al-Kuwaiti) in Abbottabad.

2009 ISI provides information about the suspicious compound in Abbottabad.

May 2009 US intelligence agencies and operatives identify a region of Pakistan where the courier Abu Ahmed al-Kuwaiti and brother were reportedly operating, but are unable to determine where they lived.

December 2009 US officials admit a "lack of intelligence" on bin Laden's location. Defense Secretary Robert Gates tells ABC that "it's been years" since there was good intelligence on this.

July 2010 An ISI official investigating Arshad Khan raises it with the Counter Terrorism Wing (CTW) of ISI and requests CIA help for satellite surveillance of Khan's residence in Abbottabad.

July US surveillance intercepts al-Kuwaiti's phone calls to known al-Qaeda associates in the cities of Kohat and Charsada in Pakistan's Khyber Pakhtunkhwa province.

August Pakistani agents working for the CIA spot al-Kuwaiti driving an SUV near the northern city of Peshawar, and begin tracking his movements.

August CIA agents follow al-Kuwaiti to a large compound in a residential sector of Abbottabad, about a kilometer from the Pakistan Military Academy.

August US President Barack Obama is briefed on a "possible lead" about the location of bin Laden.

November The ISI provides the CIA with al-Kuwaiti's cell phone number last detected in Abbottabad.

November CIA begins intensive multi-platform surveillance, including renting a nearby house, high-tech observation and eavesdropping tools and satellite imagery.

November Collective reports indicate that Abu Ahmed al-Kuwaiti, his brother (or cousin) Abrar (Saeed Ahmed) and their families are those living at the Abbottabad compound.

December CIA surveillance and intelligence conclude the Abbottabad compound has been custom-built to hide someone of significance, possibly bin Laden; they attempt to determine the identities of the inhabitants.

December CIA secures authority from Congress to "reallocate tens of millions of dollars within assorted agency budgets to fund [surveillance operations]."

In anticipation of the mission, McRaven assigned a US Navy SEAL captain "Brian" plus six other JSOC officers from his JSOC J3 Plans Cell and a CIA team from Langley, Virginia to develop plans and contingencies for "other than combined operations," that is, excluding Pakistani forces. It is evident that the CIA team would have brought with them all of their own contingency plans which were in place from the outset of their surveillance of the compound. The CIA contingency plans would have been for an immediate drone strike or assault should their surveillance have been compromised, and/or any detection that bin Laden was attempting to relocate or escape from the area.

The options

After a few weeks of research and assessment, McRaven was able to offer three courses of action: (1) a high-altitude precision bombing raid on the compound by US B-2 bombers, (2) a "direct shot" by multiple cruise missiles, and (3) a helicopter assault by US commandos.

Abbottabad is a garrison city of 1.5 million inhabitants near the capital, Islamabad. It is home to regiments of the Pakistan Army, as well as the Army's prestigious Pakistan Military Academy at Kakul. (PD)

Even a cursory understanding of the situation would indicate that options one and two were both "throwaways." Despite the risks and dangers, McRaven, a veteran US Navy SEAL tactical commander, and author of "the book" on special operations raids, could not have advocated anything else but a raid with boots on the ground. However, at that point few agreed.

In January 2011 senior White House advisor Valerie Jarrett reportedly persuaded President Obama against a commando raid option, and the (JSOC) planning team was informed. Later, the CIA reported back again, noting that there was a "sound intelligence basis" for developing courses of action to pursue bin Laden at the Abbottabad compound. At this point the commando raid options were reconsidered. Then, in late February, the President once again canceled any raid options for a second time (reportedly once again at Jarrett's urging.) Despite this, the JSOC planners continued to prepare, plan and develop raid proposals.

On March 11, 2011 the US President held the first of five National Security Council (NSC) meetings reviewing McRaven's courses of action, as well as the options taken. He again decided to wait for more certain confirmation of bin Laden's presence. Defense Secretary Gates and others doubted that bin Laden was present and discouraged risking a raid. In an NSC meeting on March 22, Gates was sceptical about a helicopter assault, and called it "too risky." USAF experts were tasked with reporting back with projections for bombing options. The options report came back at the March 29 NSC meeting with what McRaven and many others already knew. The report stated that since the CIA could not rule out the existence of an underground bunker below the compound, 32 bombs of 2,000 pounds each would be required. A bombing or missile strike would inevitably obliterate everything and leave nothing but a giant crater. Collateral damage was estimated at well over a dozen civilian casualties outside of the compound, and very little possibility of any bodies or evidence remaining to prove bin Laden's presence or death. A bombing plan was put on hold and McRaven was directed to continue developing plans for a raid.

MARCH 11, 2011

First of five US National Security Council meetings takes place

By the end of March 2010, McRaven had assembled teams of US Navy SEALs from Red Squadron to begin raid rehearsals in two US locations. Meanwhile, Abbottabad surveillance operations continued into April 2011, and a Pakistani intelligence report was filed "indicating foreigners in the surroundings of Abbottabad." Throughout the month of April 2011, the selected SEAL teams conducted rehearsals in a full-sized Abbottabad compound mock-up at Defense Testing Activity, Harvey Point, NC. They also conducted rehearsals in a high-altitude Nevada site in order to test altitude effects on the new MH-X stealth helicopters. The stealth helicopters held out at the high altitude, but the Nevada site had chain-link fences. Those at the target compound were concrete. The effect of this turned out to be an oversight that would later pose a grave threat to the entire mission.

In the April 19 NSC meeting the US President gave "provisional approval" for the raid, and Vice-Admiral McRaven was tasked with ensuring the team had "enough back-up to fight its way out of Pakistan if necessary." McRaven strengthened the mission "Exfil" contingencies to include forward staging into Pakistan of Chinook helicopters and a Quick Reaction Force.

An MH-47E Chinook flown by 160th SOAR hovers while preparing to pick up military personnel during night operations in Afghanistan. (Sgt. Daniel P. Shook/DoD)

Aerial images of the compound site in Abbottabad, Pakistan where Osama bin Laden was killed. (Left) in 2004 before construction and (right) after, in 2011. (CIA)

On April 25, McRaven and the team for *Neptune Spear* departed US Naval Air Station, Oceana, VA on C-17 aircraft. They refueled at Ramstein Air Base, Germany and landed at Bagram Air Base, Afghanistan. The team began to conduct final preparations and practice at a one-acre compound replica built at Camp Alpha at Bagram Air Base, Afghanistan, and then relocated to the forward operations base at Jalalabad, Afghanistan. CIA Director Leon Panetta met with aides and concluded that (a) they had significant "circumstantial evidence" of bin Laden's presence, (b) they had 60–80% confidence in this, and (c) the evidence was strong enough to risk the raid.

Admiral Mullen, Chairman of the Joint Chiefs of Staff (CJCS), presented the president and the NSC with the final plan for Operation *Neptune Spear* on April 28, 2011. Most advisors supported the raid. It was opposed by Vice-President Biden and Secretary of Defense Gates (who reportedly changed his mind the next day). The President told Vice-Admiral McRaven, "I'm not going to tell you what my decision is now. I'm going to go back and think about it some more." He later spoke directly to McRaven, who reported that his team was ready, and that current low moonlight conditions were good for the raid.

APRIL 29, 2011

Approval is given for Operation *Neptune Spear* to go ahead

On the morning of April 29, CIA Director Leon Panetta received a phone call from a White House aide giving verbal approval to launch Operation *Neptune Spear*. He recorded the order as received in a handwritten memorandum for record, which read:

THE FINAL COUNTDOWN TO *NEPTUNE SPEAR*

April 24 WikiLeaks reveal reports from the detainee Abu Faraj al-Libi mentioning the name Maulawi Abd al-Khaliq Jan, potentially compromising US efforts and expediting the raid plans.

April 26–27 *Neptune Spear* team conducts final practice at a one-acre compound replica built at Camp Alpha, Bagram Air Base, Afghanistan.

April 29, 0820 EDT A signed order with approval to launch Operation *Neptune Spear* is delivered to the CIA.

April 30 A 24-hour halt is placed on the mission by the President. The White House later claims this delay was due to "cloudy weather." The USAF Combat Meteorological Center's weather reports show this claim to be false. The delay allows for preparation of post-mission media releases.

May 1, 1322 EDT CIA Director Leon Panetta, acting on the President's orders, directs Vice-Admiral McRaven to proceed with the operation.

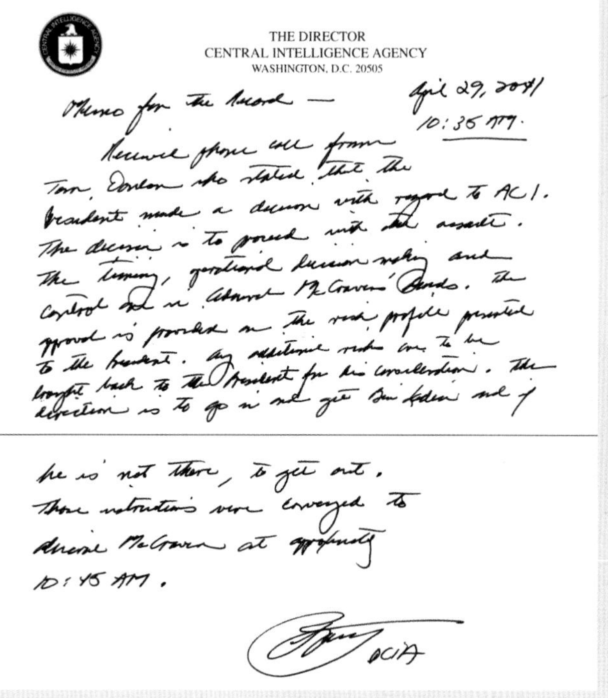
THE DIRECTOR
CENTRAL INTELLIGENCE AGENCY
WASHINGTON, D.C. 20505

Memo for the Record — April 29, 2011
10:35 AM.

Received phone call from Tom Donilon who stated that the President made a decision with regard to AC1. The decision is to proceed with the assault. The timing, operational decision making and control are in Admiral McRaven's hands. The approval is provided on the risk profile presented to the President. Any additional risks are to be brought back to the President for his consideration. The direction is to go in and get bin Laden and if he is not there, to get out. Those instructions were conveyed to Admiral McRaven at approximately 10:45 AM.

DCIA

Leon Panetta's handwritten Memo for the Record, recording the approval for the launching of Operation *Neptune Spear*. (US Government)

MEMO FOR THE RECORD Apr. 29, 2011, 10:35 a.m.

Received phone call from Tom Donilon who stated that the President made a decision with regard to AC1 [Abbottabad Compound 1]. The decision is to proceed with the assault. The timing, operational decision-making and control are in Vice-Admiral McRaven's hands. The approval is provided on the risk profile presented to the President. Any additional risks are to be brought back to the President for his consideration. The direction is to go in and get bin Laden and if he is not there, to get out. Those instructions were conveyed to Vice-Admiral McRaven at approximately 10:45 am.

Leon Panetta, DCIA

Within ten minutes of receiving the call, and after carefully documenting the action, Panetta had passed these instructions on to Vice-Admiral McRaven, and directed him to "proceed with the assault." Operation *Neptune Spear* had finally been given the go-ahead.

THE PLAN

For the security of current and future special operations and operatives, the operational plans for *Neptune Spear* have been kept classified. However, extensive open source documentation and surviving participant accounts make most aspects readily evident. What follows compiles the declassified, publically released and/or leaked, and the most evident hypotheses for Operation *Neptune Spear*.

It was to be a small raid, in that a mere 24 assaulters would be sent into just one house to get just one man. Yet, in entirety, Operation *Neptune Spear* would be immense, both in importance and scale. As the high-profile mission of the century, the execution, support and contingency plans for *Neptune Spear* employed all of the most effective national military and intelligence community resources the United States of America could bring to bear. To succeed, a mission of such scope and magnitude would require a sound plan devised with meticulous attention to detail.

The McRaven model

By January of 2011, Vice-Admiral William H. McRaven's JSOC J3 Plans Cell and a team of CIA specialists had devised the initial operational plans and contingencies for what would be called Operation *Neptune Spear*, the raid to kill or capture Osama bin Laden. Given its high priority, Vice-Admiral McRaven ensured that plans for the raid were researched and composed by his most trusted staff, were developed under his most ardent scrutiny and were formulated to comply meticulously with his own "special operation model," which is outlined in his book *Spec Ops*. McRaven lists six principles: simplicity, security, repetition, surprise, speed and purpose – or, as McRaven concisely cites them, "A simple plan, carefully concealed, repeatedly and realistically rehearsed and executed with surprise, speed and purpose." His plan also no doubt complied with the US military's *Doctrine for Joint Special Operations* [Joint Pub 3-05] and multiple other US Department of Defense standards and manuals for conducting special operations.

Vice-Admiral McRaven clearly required that these principles were strictly adhered to during *Neptune Spear*'s planning phases, the first and foremost being the principle of simplicity. The McRaven model for special operations cites three elements of simplicity that are critical to the success of a mission: limiting the number of objectives, good intelligence and innovation. The intent of applying these principles was to successfully reduce the risk to and vulnerability of the raiding forces, and enable them to succeed by achieving and maintaining relative superiority over the enemy.

Tactical objectives

The tactical objectives for Operation *Neptune Spear* were limited to those vital to mission success. There were just two: firstly, the primary objective was to "kill or capture" Osama bin Laden, and return with his body for final positive identification and disposal; and secondly, the secondary objective was to conduct sensitive site exploitation (SSE) and recover all possible documents, electronic data, hardware and materials for intelligence evaluation.

Other alternate tasks were cited, but they were not considered as vital objectives. These comprised the following; neutralize bin Laden's male al-Qaeda associates and bodyguards living in the compound; minimize any casualties among the non-combatant occupants; avoid interaction, damage or casualties with all Pakistani military and noncombatants; and minimize any risk of friendly casualties or capture.

The aerial plan

While the assault plan was (according to Vice-Admiral McRaven) a "straightforward raid," the aerial assets deployed in support of Operation *Neptune Spear* would include far more aircraft than just two stealth helicopters. With an ongoing war to cover their air activity, these aircraft would be within easy reach of the operation and able to act or react in support of the operation.

The primary aircraft for the mission, carrying the SEAL assault teams, would be two MH-X stealth helicopters of the US Army's 160th Special Operations Aviation Regiment (SOAR). The secondary aircraft (also of the 160th SOAR) served as the mission's Quick Reaction Force and consisted of two large MH-47E Chinook helicopters (QRF-1 and QRF-2) with the added firepower of their M134 miniguns. A third Contingency Force comprised two more SOAR MH-47E Chinooks (CF-1 and CF-2), carrying another 25 SEAL assaulters with the same medical and re-supply support; they would fly to a pre-positioned staging point just inside the Afghanistan border.

Several USAF combat search-and-rescue aircraft and teams were staged in nearby support positions. These teams were "on-call" from the start to provide emergency rescue or extraction if needed, and able to react at any point during the mission. In addition, an E-6A Mercury airborne command post would be in the air over Afghanistan to ensure there was no break in the continuous command control and communications between all of the elements.

To get the 24 SEALs into Abbottabad, do the job, and return safely required dozens of aircraft – to transport, protect, observe, and support – all of which were coordinated by an E-3 Sentry. This E-3 is here seen being refueled by a KC-10 Extender over Afghanistan, on another long mission. (SSgt Greg Biondo/USAF)

The entire aerial part of the mission would be under the watchful eye and protection of an E-3 Sentry Airborne Warning and Control System (AWACS) aircraft. The E-3 capabilities included all-weather electronic surveillance, tracking all friendly aircraft, looking for any non-friendly aircraft, detecting any Pakistani radar, electronic communications or air defense activity, and full ability to counter any non-friendly communications, detection or weapon systems if necessary.

Several unmanned aerial vehicles (UAVs), including RQ-4 Global Hawk and RQ-170 Sentinel, would be launched and fly undetected over Pakistan for the duration of the operation. Aside from being able to provide immediate missile strike support to the assaulters, these would also provide live-feed video surveillance and a relay/back-up to audio communications where needed.

In addition, satellite, airborne and ground-deployed electronic warfare assets would be fully active, including highly classified signal intelligence multi-spectrum intercept and jamming capabilities. These would all be fully operational and monitoring all aspects of Pakistani military and other activities for any hint of detection, reaction or possible cause for alarm. Also, US advisors to the Pakistan Air Force (PAF) would be instructed to monitor and report any activity of Pakistani F-16 jets.

Several F/A-18 Super Hornet fighter jets would be airborne and "on station" to provide air support. As the mission kicked off their fuel would be "topped off" by KC-135 Stratotanker refueling aircraft. US Air Force stealth aircraft would also be available to penetrate Pakistani airspace undetected if their employment became critically necessary. AH-64A Apache attack helicopters were available inside the Afghanistan border. The Apaches' accurate long-range firepower could provide overwhelming direct fire support for any emergency, or to cover any contested extraction mission if necessary. On the ground in Afghanistan, several companies of US Army infantrymen with helicopter lift assets were on call and available as an emergency force able to travel to the border areas and provide heavy firepower and additional ground force reinforcement if needed.

Several C-130 Hercules transport aircraft would be at the Jalalabad airstrip to take the assault team, JSOC, CIA and support elements to and from their quarters in the JSOC compound at Bagram Air Base. Finally, a V-22 Osprey would be standing by at Bagram to transport bin Laden's body to the aircraft carrier CVN-70 USS *Carl Vinson* in the northern Arabian Sea. Before any assault elements lifted off the ground, this full array of US aircraft would be airborne and "on station" in the skies over Afghanistan.

The assault plan

The primary assaulters for Operation *Neptune Spear* would be 24 US Navy SEALs, a dog, and one interpreter/operative. In all, over 79 Special Operations commandos were to be dedicated to the mission, supported by a dozen or more helicopters, pilots and crews, hundreds of unknowing ground support personnel, over 20 fixed-wing combat and combat support aircraft, plus multiple intelligence and surveillance operator teams.

To become a SEAL, volunteers go through the 24-week "Basic Underwater Demolition/SEAL" training and assessment program. The first phase of training is designed to test the candidates' extreme fitness and endurance. Week Three is "Hell Week." The Hell Week program puts candidates through more than 20 hours of physical training every day and extremes of cold and wet, as these mud-covered soldiers are experiencing. (DoD)

In Pakistan, over a dozen teams of armed CIA operatives in SUV vehicles, as well as separately arranged Pakistani private security agencies, would be deployed to pre-selected locations as an on-the-ground emergency extraction option for the mission. US diplomatic stations in Pakistan would also be monitoring all activities and standing by to react as needed. Other CIA operatives in Abbottabad would "arrange" (presumably though bribery) to effect a power blackout in the area of the compound including the Pakistan Military Academy, and a concurrent mobile phone service interruption. All of this would be initiated before midnight while the assault force was en route.

The assault force would conduct final preparations and stage at the nearest secure US special operations base at Jalalabad, Afghanistan. The basic outline of the plan was for the 24 SEALs and interpreter to make the 90-minute flight over the border mountains into Pakistan undetected on two stealth helicopters, assault the compound in Abbottabad, complete the mission objectives, depart within 30 minutes and fly back to Jalalabad with bin Laden's body and all of the SSE material they could carry. JSOC planners considered a hundred different events that could possibly go wrong, developed contingency plans for those most probable and rehearsed for as many as time would allow.

The final plan called for the lead MH-X helicopter (Prince 51) to carry Chalk One composed of 10 SEAL assaulters, a sniper and the mission senior master chief. The trail MH-X (Prince 52) would carry

The SEALs would fast-rope from the MH-X helicopters, which were flown by the elite pilots of the 160th Special Operations Aviation Regiment (SOAR) into the compound. This is a night-time training exercise, fast-roping from a conventional MH-60L Black Hawk of the 160th SOAR. (Elisandro T. Diaz/US Navy)

Chalk Two, composed of 10 SEAL assaulters, another sniper, the tactical mission commander, the combat-assault dog and handler, and a Pakistani- and Arabic-speaking interpreter/operative. The rotorcraft would fly NOE (nap-of-the-earth), following the terrain through remote valleys and behind steep mountains while airborne assets would monitor any signs of Pakistani radar transmissions.

With a limited lift capability, maximum load and carrying reduced fuel weight, the two stealth helicopters would need to refuel before making the return flight to Afghanistan. Therefore, the assault flight would be followed by two slower-moving MH-47E Chinook helicopters (QRF-1 and QRF-2) carrying two fuel bladders to re-fuel the Black Hawks, a Quick Reaction Force (QRF) of 25 SEALs and support personnel, the lift capacity to extract all SSE items and any prisoners recovered from the compound, plus the added firepower of M134 miniguns on each Chinook. The two QRF Chinooks were to land in a sparsely populated area of Pakistan approximately 20 miles east of Abbottabad and deploy a small surveillance team for their own security. The pilots were to keep the aircraft prepared to take off at a moment's notice. The third Contingency Force of 25 more SEAL assaulters and support personnel would depart last and fly on two additional MH-47E Chinooks to staging points inside Afghanistan.

The two MH-Xs would approach Abbottabad from the east and avoid flying directly over or alerting the Pakistani military installations. As they

Navy SEALs conduct close-quarters combat training in a simulated house at US Navy Training Center in Moyock, North Carolina. (Eddie Harrison/ US Navy)

OPERATION *NEPTUNE SPEAR* – TASK ORGANIZATION

All elements in the operation were temporarily transferred to the authority of the CIA. *Neptune Spear* involved a total of 79 special operations assaulters and/or specialists, including many US Navy SEALs from Red Squadron, US Naval Special Warfare Development Group (NSWDG, or DEVGRU), and special operations support specialists from Joint Special Operations Command.

Chalk One (12) – Callsign: "Prince 51"*
Mission Senior Master Chief (1)
Team A: Team Leader and four Assaulters (includes medical and demolition specialists) (5)
Team B: Team Leader and four Assaulters (includes alternate interpreter) (5)
Chalk One Airborne Sniper (1)

Chalk Two (13) – Callsign "Prince 52"*
Mission Commanding Officer (1)
Team C: Team Leader and four Assaulters (includes medical and demolition specialists) (5)
Team D: Team Leader and four Assaulters (includes one dog handler) (5)
Chalk Two Airborne Sniper (1)
Interpreter/Operative (1)
Combat assault dog: Cairo

* Note: The "Prince 51" and "52" aircraft call-signs as identified by the researchers for the *Zero Dark Thirty* screenplay are used herein to facilitate this account.

Quick Reaction Force (QRF)
MH-47E Chinook (2), with:
QRF Commander (1)
QRF Senior Chief (1)
4x SEAL assault teams (5 each)
Fuel Specialists (2)
Interpreter/Operative (1)
Chinook crew (3–4)

Contingency Force (CF)
MH-47E Chinook (2), with:
CF Commander (1)
CF Senior Chief (1)
4x SEAL assault teams (5 each)
Medical Team (2)
Chinook crew (3–4)

Deployed in Pakistan
Security and medical specialists from US diplomatic stations in Pakistan – on alert
Emergency ground evacuation element: *c.* 10 vehicles, CIA operatives and medics
Pakistani private contractor security elements *c.* 4 personnel and 2 vehicles

approached, CIA operatives would "paint" the bin Laden compound with a target laser pointer to ensure the pilots made no mistake in selecting the correct target.

Prince 52 would land first at the road intersection just north-east of the compound and insert four members of Chalk Two: Cairo and his handler, the interpreter and a SEAL security man with each. The interpreter and a SEAL would establish a security post at the road intersection to keep any vehicles or locals from approaching. The dog team would immediately move to patrol the compound perimeter, with Cairo sniffing for any sign of human activity.

Meanwhile the Prince 51 stealth helicopter would briefly hover over the compound to insert 11 assaulters by fast-rope down into courtyard A. Prince 52 would follow and place its remaining nine assaulters directly onto the roof of the compound's main building. Afterwards, both MH-Xs would draw back and begin circling the compound, taking turns (using the SEAL sniper on board) to cover the assaulters on the objective.

Once inserted inside the compound, Chalk Two assaulters would drop down onto the third floor balcony and begin to clear the main house from

Aviation elements

Rotorcraft:

2x MH-X Advanced Special Operations helicopters, 160th Special Operations Aviation Regiment (SOAR)
4x MH-47E Chinook helicopters, 160th SOAR
4x US Air Force Combat Search and Rescue helicopters and teams
4x AH-64A Apache attack helicopters

Surveillance and munitions-capable unmanned aerial vehicles (UAVs):

RQ-4 Global Hawk
RQ-170 Sentinel
MQ-9 Reaper

Fixed-wing aircraft:

F/A-18 Super Hornets – fighters aboard USS *Carl Vinson* (CVN-70) in the North Arabian Sea
E-6A Mercury – airborne command post
E-3 Sentry – airborne warning and control system (AWACS)
KC-135 Stratotanker – refueling aircraft
C-130 Hercules – general transport
V-22 Osprey – to transport body of target post-operation

MH-X ASOH – the "stealth helicopter"

One of the most interesting revelations (in terms of technological innovation) to come out of Operation *Neptune Spear* is the deployment of the MH-X Advanced Special Operations Helicopter – although, being classified, the aircraft's name and existence have been neither officially confirmed nor officially denied. While silent-running helicopter blades had been employed by special operations forces for some time in Afghanistan and Iraq, *Neptune Spear* was the first known operational use of a tactical helicopter with radar-defeating stealth capabilities. The MH-X ASOH is a highly classified version of the most modern Sikorsky UH-60 Black Hawk, a twin-engine, medium-lift military helicopter. The MH-X, commonly referred to as the "stealth helicopter," is a heavily modified version of the UH-60 that incorporates state of the art stealth and noise-reduction technology.

Silent running features: Additional tail and main rotor blades, allowing slower rotation and reduced noise. The main rotor blades are arrayed in an offset pattern, and the tail and main rotors are specially shaped and covered – both of which help reduce noise.

Reduced radar detection features: The overall shape helps absorb radar waves or bounces them off in different directions. Both the front and rear retractable landing gear reduce the radar signature. The helicopter is coated in a smooth material that absorbs radar waves and inhibits infrared sensor detection. The tailboom has been extended and enlarged to help avoid radar reflection. A cover on the main and rear rotor heads shields machinery from radar reflection. Rivets are recessed and covered to avoid radar wave sensitivity.

the top down, hypothetically getting bin Laden in the first few moments. Chalk One assaulters would clear the guesthouse, begin to secure the first floor of the main building and allow Chalk Two to work its way down.

All assault teams were to search and clear every room, closet and compartment in the entire compound. The gate would also be opened to bring Cairo and handler inside to search the compound for hidden people or stashed materials. Once all targets were neutralized and the entire compound secured, an observing local CIA operative would give the word for electrical power to resume, facilitating SSE. All electronic equipment and documents were to be gathered for intelligence analysis, placed in bags and taken away. Any noncombatants were to be searched for weapons, explosives or suicide vests and then placed under guard.

The assault leaders were tasked with conducting initial visual identification and confirmation on bin Laden's body and the mission commander was instructed to transmit a codeword once for achieving the objective: Geronimo. Team leaders were designated to take digital photos of bin Laden as well as taking DNA samples on site, in case his body could not be evacuated for any reason. The MH-47E Chinook QRF-1 was on call to

US Navy V-22 Osprey tiltrotor aircraft such as this were pre-staged and kept on standby both for long-range force extraction contingencies and/or to fly the body of Osama bin Laden to the US fleet in the Arabian Sea, where an autopsy, DNA identification and burial at sea would be conducted from the aircraft carrier USS *Carl Vinson*. (Lauren G. Randall/US Navy)

aid in Exfil and pick up any casualties, all SSE and some of the assault team to alleviate additional load weight in the stealth helicopters. Once the aircraft were uploaded, they were to depart immediately.

The MH-Xs were to meet with the Chinooks at the refuel point, and once refueled all aircraft were to depart for their return flight to Afghanistan. Immediately upon safe departure of the aircraft, the CIA operatives in Abbottabad would abandon the compound, send all security teams home for the night, and initiate egress of operatives out of the country.

The body of Osama bin Laden, and all captured intelligence would be collected and processed as soon as the teams arrived back at Jalalabad. The entire force was to fly from Jalalabad to Bagram and conduct a post-mission debriefing while bin Laden's body was to be flown in a V-22 Osprey from Bagram to the aircraft carrier USS *Carl Vinson* in the northern Arabian Sea. Genetic specialists were prepared to conduct DNA evaluations to confirm that the dead body was that of bin Laden.

THE RAID

On May 2, 2011, after many months of planning, preparation and rehearsals, as well as political delays and multiple cancellations, Operation *Neptune Spear* was finally launched. Vice-Admiral William H. McRaven would direct the raid from Jalalabad Tactical Operations Center. Command centers would also monitor the raid from the US Embassy in Islamabad, the Pentagon and CIA HQ Langley, Virginia. The US President Barack Obama and selected staffers would also monitor the CIA feeds in a White House briefing room.

At about 2315 hours local time, the two stealth helicopters took off with the assault force from Jalalabad in Afghanistan. Within 15 minutes the two MH-Xs had crossed the international border and entered Pakistani air space undetected. The two aircraft hugged the earth as they flew east above the hilly terrain. No sightings of them were reported in the sparsely populated areas, and every 15 minutes the pilots advised that they "had not been painted," that is, Pakistani radar had not picked them up.

A few minutes after the departure of the MH-Xs, two MH-47E Chinooks also took off from Jalalabad, carrying the Quick Reaction Force (QRF), followed by the Contingency Force (CF) in two more Chinooks soon after. They all flew to their staging points as planned, without incident. Meanwhile, USAF combat search-and-rescue teams took up their operational positions.

The air assets supporting the operations were all already in place, assisted by an E-6A Mercury airborne command post. F/A-18 Super Hornet fighter jets were fully fueled "on station." Surveillance and munitions-capable UAV drones, including the RQ-4 Global Hawk and the RQ-170 Sentinel, remained in the air over Afghanistan and Pakistan undetected for the duration of the operation.

MAY 2, 2011
Operation *Neptune Spear* is launched

Additional rotorcraft, including a flight of AH-64A Apache attack helicopters were all in position within Afghanistan to provide added transportation and fire support, or to react to any emergency or extraction needs as necessary. E-3 Sentry (AWACS) began monitoring and tracking all aircraft, detecting Pakistani

The operation's forward area refueling point (FARP) relied on the micro-FARE (forward area refueling equipment) system. This refueling system can be used with a UH-60 Black Hawk or a CH-47 Chinook, which are respectively nicknamed the 'Fat Hawk' and the 'Fat Cow' when used in this role. The system can be set up in 15 minutes. Refueling can take longer, depending on how many gallons are needed. (Sgt. Daniel Schroeder/US Army)

electronic activity and communications, augmented by satellite, airborne and ground-deployed electronic warfare (EW) elements.

CIA operatives in teams were deployed in Pakistan and standing by to support the mission, as was the US diplomatic mission there. As planned, a mobile phone service interruption and power blackout commenced in the area of the target compound, including the Pakistan Military Academy. At this late hour of the night, very few took notice. Such interruptions were a common occurrence.

By about 0030 hours local time, the two MH-47E Chinooks of the QRF stopped near Kandar (Hassanzai), a sparsely populated area on the left bank of the River Indus, and approximately 20 miles west of Abbottabad. The two Chinooks established a forward area refueling point (FARP) adjacent to a farmer's field. They off-loaded a small surveillance team for their own security, while all others remained on board. The pilots kept the aircraft prepared to take off at a moment's notice. Local farmer Abdul Munaf witnessed them landing near his crops and assumed they were Pakistanis. As he approached the helicopters, SEALs captured and detained him to avoid compromising their mission.

The "Infil"

The two stealth helicopters flew in over Abbottabad from the east and avoided flying directly over, and thus alerting, the Pakistani military installations. By about 0055 hours, as they approached the neighborhood, operatives "painted" the bin Laden compound with a laser pointer to ensure there was no mistaking the correct target. Both rotorcraft slowed to a hover.

The Chalk Two MH-X quickly landed and dropped four SEALs, the interpreter and the SEAL dog handler next to the road intersection just north of the compound. As the Chalk Two helicopter quickly re-ascended, the interpreter and one SEAL set up a security position at the road intersection to keep all vehicles or persons from approaching. The other two SEALs and Cairo the dog hurried toward the compound, circling clockwise, with the dog preparing to sniff out anyone who might attempt to escape.

Meanwhile, the Chalk One helicopter (flown by a pilot only referred to as "Teddy") flew over the compound and began to hover. Twelve SEAL assaulters prepared to fast-rope down into the courtyard. US Navy SEAL Mark Owen (an alias) was first at the door.

Chalk One down

At this vulnerable point, the meticulously composed plan met a serious and unanticipated setback that placed the entire operation in jeopardy. Whilst hovering some 30–40ft in the air, and with the engines and rotor blades fully engaged, the Chalk One stealth helicopter rapidly lost lift power. The pilot struggled as the Chalk One bird shuddered, tilted and failed to respond. The aircraft was suffering from something called a "hazardous airflow vortex." The vortex was caused, in this case, by hovering directly over the multiple, enclosed, high concrete walls of the compound. The MH-X's lift capacity

This scale model of the Abbottabad compound was used to plan the raid. With fields carved out of clay and the building's walls made of foam-core, the model was built in six weeks by a special team at the National Geospatial-Intelligence Agency. (AFP/Getty Images)

TACTICAL MISSION TIMELINE, OPERATION *NEPTUNE SPEAR* PHASE 1

All times are local time.

2330, May 1 Operation *Neptune Spear* is launched. Two stealth helicopters of 160th SOAR, carrying 24 SEALs from Red Squadron, initiate a 90-minute flight from Jalalabad to Abbottabad. Two Chinook helicopters follow the MH-Xs into Pakistan carrying extra fuel for the MH-Xs and a QRF of 24 SEALs. A Contingency Force of two Chinooks and 25 SEALs are pre-positioned just inside the Afghanistan border to provide additional reinforcements if needed during the raid.

0001, May 2 The two MH-Xs cross into Pakistan undetected.

0030 The QRF Chinooks land in a deserted area of Pakistan approximately 20 miles east of Abbottabad, and remain on standby.

0045 CIA operatives in Abbottabad create a power blackout, and mobile-phone service disconnects in the area, including in the Pakistan Military Academy.

0055 The two MH-Xs approach Abbottabad from east and slow to a hover.

0058 The Chalk Two bird drops four SEALs, an interpreter and a dog handler by the road intersection northeast of the compound, to secure the perimeter.

0057 The Chalk One bird attempts to hover and suffers a hazardous airflow vortex, loses lift and crashes in E Courtyard, with its tail resting across the south wall. No-one is injured. The SEALs exit immediately.

0059 The Chalk Two pilot decides to land north of the compound, and deploys the team leader and six SEALs.

was already limited by the stealth design, and it immediately became clear to the pilot that they were going down hard. For brief moment the crew faced straight down at the ground. A hard landing in an open field could be dangerous enough, but collision with a concrete wall would be fatal. Once the spinning rotors met with an unmoving mass, centrifugal force would tear the helicopter apart, cause an explosion and kill or wound everyone on board – and the mission would have been over before it started. The pilot had a fraction of a second to react, regain some partial control and avoid disintegration of both the aircraft and Operation *Neptune Spear*.

Rather than follow a natural reaction to attempt to power-up against the loss of lift, "Teddy" kept his composure and coolly followed his training and experience. He allowed the bird to slip down toward the open "E Courtyard" in an effort to avoid a dangerous rotor-impact with any of the buildings or walls. The tail section failed to clear the east wall and settled on top of it, and the MH-X's nose dug into the soft plowed soil of the courtyard's garden.

After impact, the helicopter crew chief shouted "Go! Go!," ordering the SEALs to exit and clear away from the aircraft immediately. As they did so, the pilot used what little remaining lift control he could garner to continue balancing the aircraft between the wall and its nose on the ground, keeping the rotors level and away from any obstructions. As he did this, the rotor blade tips were digging into the courtyard dirt and kicking a great deal of debris and dust into the air all around them. The pilot and copilot began shutdown procedures for the helicopter as it came to rest without tipping to either side. The MH-X and Chalk One were now on the ground safely, inside the compound, thanks to the unflappable nerves and elite flying skills of "Teddy" and his crew from the 160th SOAR "Night Stalkers."

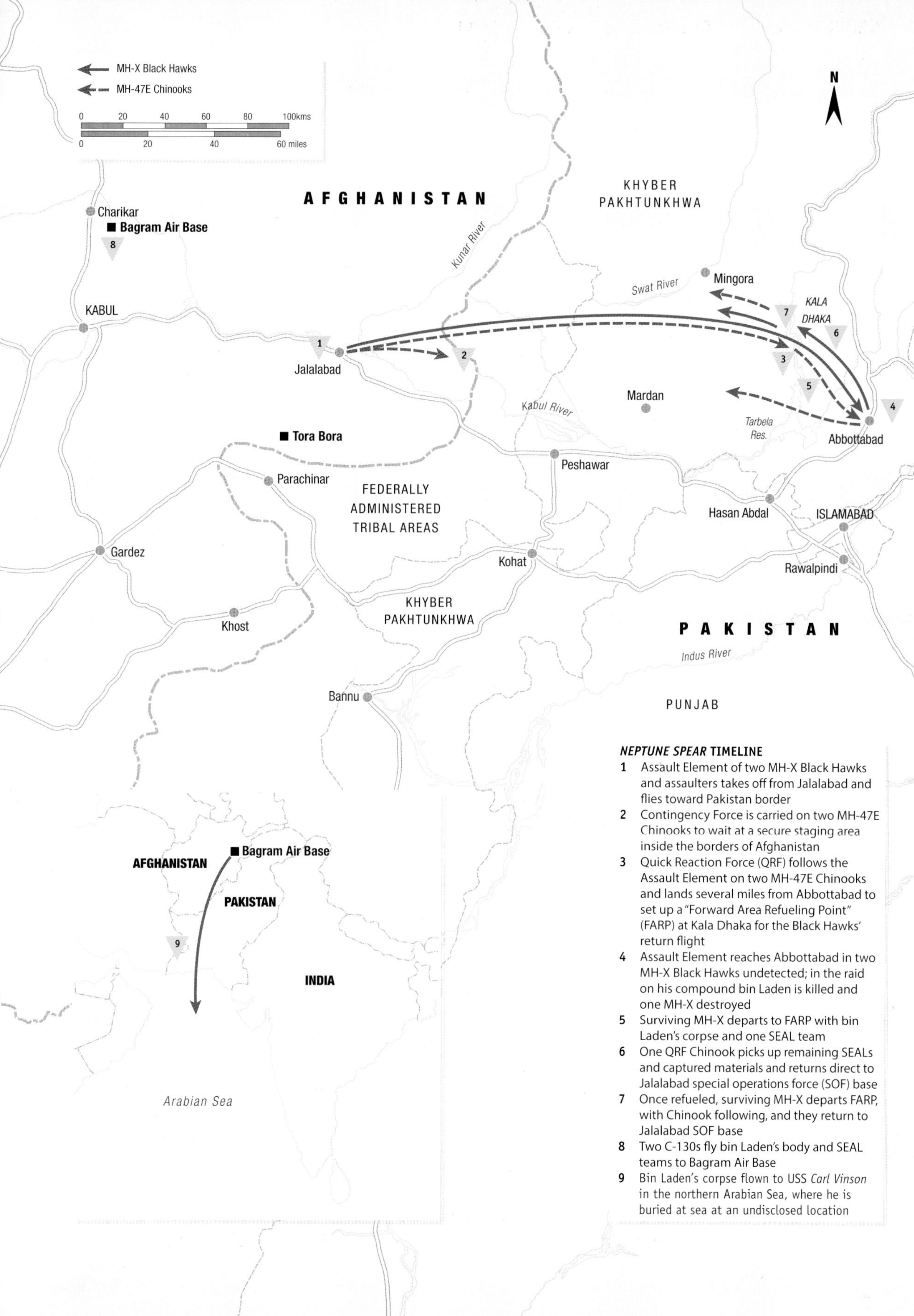

NEPTUNE SPEAR TIMELINE

1. Assault Element of two MH-X Black Hawks and assaulters takes off from Jalalabad and flies toward Pakistan border
2. Contingency Force is carried on two MH-47E Chinooks to wait at a secure staging area inside the borders of Afghanistan
3. Quick Reaction Force (QRF) follows the Assault Element on two MH-47E Chinooks and lands several miles from Abbottabad to set up a "Forward Area Refueling Point" (FARP) at Kala Dhaka for the Black Hawks' return flight
4. Assault Element reaches Abbottabad in two MH-X Black Hawks undetected; in the raid on his compound bin Laden is killed and one MH-X destroyed
5. Surviving MH-X departs to FARP with bin Laden's corpse and one SEAL team
6. One QRF Chinook picks up remaining SEALs and captured materials and returns direct to Jalalabad special operations force (SOF) base
7. Once refueled, surviving MH-X departs FARP, with Chinook following, and they return to Jalalabad SOF base
8. Two C-130s fly bin Laden's body and SEAL teams to Bagram Air Base
9. Bin Laden's corpse flown to USS *Carl Vinson* in the northern Arabian Sea, where he is buried at sea at an undisclosed location

To the heart of the compound

One of the lead Red Squadron assaulters, Mark Owen, had raced forward away from the Chalk One helicopter and did not look back. He stopped in the far southern corner of the courtyard, farthest away from the main compound. The next eleven assaulters reached the ground, took up a tactical posture, began to move north along the wall (under the balanced aircraft), and toward the compound's main buildings.

It was about this time that an Abbottabad resident, IT consultant Sohaib Athar (who evidently had power and an internet connection in his neighborhood) sent out live, real-time broadcasts over Twitter. His first tweet at 0058 (Abbottabad time) stated: "Helicopter hovering above Abbottabad at 1AM (is a rare event)."

Upon witnessing the Chalk One bird's problem, and hearing the pilot's radio report, the Chalk Two pilot decided to implement a contingency option. He landed in the field just northwest of the compound and deployed the assault team leader and six more remaining assaulters there. An alternate entry plan had been to use explosives to open up a small gate in the northwest corner of the main compound. Once the Chalk Two bird had taken off, the SEALs immediately moved toward the designated gate and prepared it for breaching.

Meanwhile, inside the compound things became quieter again. The Chalk One assaulters deployed inside Courtyard E found the only gate securely locked. They stacked up against the wall, while their designated demo man quickly conducted a breach of the courtyard gate with a small explosive charge. The group leader warned the other elements over the radio before detonating. The gate blew with a sharp bang that echoed through the night.

Once the gate had been blown, the Chalk One lead assaulter pried the metal door back while others began to pass into the narrow driveway and toward the guesthouse. One Chalk 1 sniper (who should have still been airborne aboard Chalk One's bird at this time) climbed onto a shed's roof to cover the advancing Chalk One assaulters. Despite a crashing helicopter and gate demolition, no activity was detected and no one had (yet) opened fire.

The SEALs from Chalk Two detonated their explosive charge on the northwest gate. After the detonation, they quickly radioed to all, "Failed breach." They found an unexpected surprise behind the blown gate: the doorway was completely bricked in. The next alternate entry plan was to breach the main gate on the west side of the compound. The SEALs moved toward the gate and prepared another charge. It was now 0104 hours.

Meanwhile, the Chalk One SEALs had approached the guesthouse, and found the door locked. As Mark Owen kneeled to the side and attempted to tape an explosive charge to the door handle, the first gunshots of the night rang out from behind the door. It was the telltale crack of an AK-47 assault rifle. A flurry of AK-47 bullets flew past Owen. One of the AK-47 rounds struck the handle of the bolt–cutters strapped to his back. It was a close call, as the handle only protruded a few inches above his shoulder and neck.

Even before the AK-47 fire ceased, the SEAL assaulters covering Owen had fired their suppressed weapons in a steady stream of carefully placed rounds through the door and into the approximate origin of the AK-47 fire. All noise ceased, and they called for those in the house to come out. A woman opened the door, came out and said, "He is dead. You killed him." She was quickly cuffed and led aside.

MAY 2, 0105 HOURS

Abu Ahmed al-Kuwaiti is shot dead on the ground floor

Just inside the doorway, the SEALs found the dead body of bin Laden's courier Abu Ahmed al-Kuwaiti – or, more correctly, that of Ibrahim Saeed Ahmed. The assaulters quickly cleared the house and found al-Kuwaiti's children. All of them were placed in a back room. The Chalk One sniper re-deployed onto the guesthouse roof, and covered the Chalk One SEALs' advance back into the courtyard and toward the main house. It was 0105 hours.

Once the crashed MH-X had completely shut down, the crew inspected their aircraft and found only superficial damage. They considered attempting to get it airborne again, but decided that the damaged aircraft could be too risky to operate safely. The pilots and crew began to recover all classified items from the aircraft and obtained permission to prepare it for demolition. Soon after this, one of the QRF Chinooks was ordered dispatched to participate in the "Exfil," to replace the crashed stealth helicopter.

After hearing the small-arms fire, the overall mission SEAL team commander, who was with Chalk One outside the compound, transmitted over the mission radio net that he was going to breach the main gate to gain access. The team's Senior Chief Petty Officer, "Chief Mike," immediately responded from inside the compound, "Belay that!" (a nautical term for "cancel that order!") and advised the commander "I am inside and will let you in." Chief Mike then walked 30ft to the main gate and unlocked it from the inside.

Chalk One then entered the compound and joined Chalk Two with assaulters "stacked up" on both the north and south doors of the main house. Few of the SEALs were now in position to assault in the order and locations prescribed by their primary assignments. Since they had all repeatedly rehearsed multiple contingencies for this the mission, each man knew what to do.

One night in Abbottabad (overleaf)

This scene depicts the recovery from the potentially disastrous mission failure that occurred just after 0057 hours, when the MH-X pilot avoided a catastrophic crash and made a hard landing into bin Laden's garden, "E Courtyard," and the aircraft's nose dug into the soft dirt. The pilot can be seen quickly shutting down the aircraft's rotors as he balances the rotor tail on top of the 9ft-high concrete security wall. Rotor blade tips beat into the courtyard dirt and kicked up a great deal of debris and dust. With no one injured, the crew chief shouted "GO! GO!" and the squadron assaulters jumped clear of the aircraft into an offensive tactical posture.

The first man to exit was SEAL "Mark Owen" (seen to the right, with sleeves cut off just below the arm pockets). He jumped out of the crashing helicopter and sprinted to the south corner of courtyard E without looking back. The other assaulters reached the ground and immediately began moving in the opposite direction toward the compound's main buildings. Within seconds the helicopter was stabilized and shutting down. The team redirected focus toward the main buildings and the mission objective: Osama bin Laden. Some of the SEALs carry the Heckler & Koch (HK) MP7a1 submachine gun with 40-round magazine, night vision scope, infrared laser pointer, white-light torch and silencer. Other SEALS carry the HK 416 (5.56mm) assault rifle with 10.4in barrel. At least one SEAL sniper is on this team with a 7.62mm HK 417 with 12in barrel, sniper-scope and night vision adapter, Harris bipod and silencer. As seen here, every SEAL is packing a 9mm Sig Sauer P226 pistol with silencer in a leg holster, along with extra ammunition, as a secondary firearm.

SHUMATE
2013

In the main building, several SEALs had entered the south door, and on the first floor encountered al-Kuwaiti's brother Abrar al-Kuwaiti, who was reportedly armed. With the power still out, it was pitch black inside the main building, but the SEALs could see clearly with their night vision devices. The SEALs shot and killed Abrar and his wife Bushra in the doorway to a first floor room. The SEALs continued to clear each room on the first floor. They again found several children, whom they moved into a side room on the first floor.

At the far end of the center hallway they found a large metal door blocking entry into the stairwell. It was heavy and firmly locked. They decided against a breach attempt there, and went outside the building and around to join the others entering from the far side door.

The SEALs' DEVGRU insignia. The operation's codename, *Neptune Spear*, reflected their trident emblem. (US Navy)

"Geronimo – EKIA"

Slowly SEAL assaulters began to stack outside the north door, in two and three man groups. The lead group breached an interior door allowing access into the stairwell to the upper floors. The SEALs moved quietly and methodically into the building, peering into the dark.

On the second floor the point man caught a glimpse of someone running up to the third floor. The follow-on teams began clearing each room on the second floor. While covering the stairs, the point man saw and heard movement on the flight up the stairwell. He guessed it was bin Laden's 23-year-old son Khalid, and called Khalid's name. When he called a second time, a head peered around the corner of the wall. Aiming his weapon and laser pointer through the darkness, the point man fired one shot at the chin of Khalid bin Laden. The bullet went up through his head and killed him instantly. His body dropped onto the landing, and he was double-tapped in the chest as the assaulters advanced over him.

The SEALs took their time advancing up the stairwell, scanning carefully with their night vision goggles. Although they could see clearly, the third floor was in pitch darkness for its inhabitants. The lead two SEALs continued to creep up the stairwell toward the top floor. The assaulters knew Abu Ahmed al-Kuwaiti, Abrar and Khalid were already dead. The only known adult male remaining would have to be Osama bin Laden. It was just as their intelligence briefs had predicted. So far, the pre-mission intelligence details provided by the CIA had all proven to be precisely accurate.

Nearing the top of the stairs, the point man saw a male figure passing into a doorway to the third-floor bedroom on the right. He immediately fired a round, but the figure withdrew into the room.

What happened next is still unclear, and varying accounts exist.

One reported version of events suggests that the point man advanced toward the bedroom door. As he did so, two women came toward him screaming in the dark. Disregarding the threat of one or both being armed with weapons or explosive suicide vests, he grabbed both and carried them clear of his teammate, who advanced through the doorway. The women continued to scream as the second SEAL entered the bedroom. He could see bin Laden standing and holding a woman in front of him. The woman, Amal Ahmed Abdul Fatah, was bin Laden's youngest wife. The SEAL raised his weapon up and over the woman's head and squeezed off two rounds into bin Laden's head.

An alternative version – as in Mark Owen's account of the raid – states that the round fired by the point man on the landing struck bin Laden in the head, forcing bin Laden to fall backwards into the bedroom. As they entered the room, the SEALs saw two women wailing over bin Laden's twitching body. One SEAL manhandled the women out of the way, while the other shot bin Laden repeatedly in the chest to make sure he was dead. In Owen's account, bin Laden evidently did not use any of his wives as a human shield.

Whatever the truth of bin Laden's final moments, the fact remains that the job appeared to have been executed. At approximately 0109 hours local Pakistani time, Operation *Neptune Spear* had achieved its primary objective. Osama bin Laden had been shot dead by a US Navy SEAL. His body lay in the pitch blackness of his third-floor bedroom with three bullets just above his left eye. The mission, however, was far from nearing completion. Firstly, the SEALs had to make sure that this was their man. There was much else still to do, and the tactical situation was far from secure. The level of risk and vulnerability to an imminent confrontation with the Pakistani military was yet to climax.

TACTICAL MISSION TIMELINE, OPERATION *NEPTUNE SPEAR* PHASE 2

All times are local time.

0102 The Chalk One SEALs place a sniper on a shed roof, and advance to clear the guesthouse. The crashed MH-X pilot and crew destroy and remove instruments, radio and classified fixtures inside the helicopter.

0103 The Chalk Two SEALs attempt to breach the northeast gate, but find it is bricked in.

0104 The Chalk One SEALs clear the guesthouse, and kill bin Laden's courier Abu Ahmed al-Kuwaiti. A sniper deploys onto the guesthouse roof, and the SEALs proceed to the main house.

0105 The Chalk Two SEALs are given entry through the main gate (D) by "Chief Mike"; both Chalks advance to the north and south doors of the main house.

0106 SEALs enter the south door, and shoot and kill al-Kuwaiti's brother Abrar and wife Bushra. After clearing the first floor, they find the metal stairwell door firmly blocked.

0107 SEALs enter the north door, and breach the interior door into the stairwell up to second and third floors. They move methodically through the building, clearing each room and floor.

0108 SEALs clear the second floor and media rooms. The point man shoots and kills Khalid bin Laden as he peers down the stairwell.

0109 SEALs advance up the stairwell towards the third floor bedroom and shoot bin Laden dead. Amal Ahmed Abdul Fatah, one of bin Laden's wives, is also wounded.

The two SEALs were alone with Osama and his family only for a few seconds. Having advanced upstairs alone, all of the other assaulters were still below, cautiously clearing each of the rooms, compartments and closets on the larger second floor, with each group carefully covering one

THE "INFIL"

MAY 2, 2011

EVENTS

1 On approach, Chalk Two MH-X helicopter inserts two SEALs, the interpreter, and the dog handler next to the road intersection just north of the compound

2 Chalk One MH-X helicopter attempts to hover to allow 12 assaulters to fast-rope down into the courtyard. But it rapidly loses lift power in a "hazardous airflow vortex" and makes a hard landing on the wall, inside courtyard E

3 Chalk One SEAL "Mark Owen" exits the aircraft to the south as the pilot balances the aircraft between the wall and the ground, keeping rotors level and away from obstructions

4 The other 11 Chalk One assaulters exit the aircraft and move toward the main building

5 Chalk Two pilot opts not to risk potential "hazardous airflow vortex" and inserts the team commander and remainder of Chalk Two SEALs onto a field near the compound

6 Chalk One SEALs breach locked gate between Courtyard E and driveway, and team deploys sniper to cover over the wall, and towards the compound's main building

7 Two assaulters and Cairo the dog circle around the compound clockwise, searching and sniffing for any potential escape route, or anyone who might attempt to escape

8 Chalk One SEALs approach guesthouse and receive AK-47 fire through the door. Their return fire kills bin Laden's courier Abu Ahmed al-Kuwaiti. SEALs clear the house and detain al-Kuwaiti's wife and children inside

9 Chalk Two SEALs attempt to breach compound wall from outside, but the wall is bricked in and the attempt fails. Team's Senior Chief Petty Officer opens main game and lets Chalk Two in

10 Chalk One SEALs enter south door to main building, shoot and kill al-Kuwaiti's brother Abrar al-Kuwaiti and his wife. Ground floor is cleared, and women and children secured

11 Chalks One and Two conduct forced entry into main building from opposite side

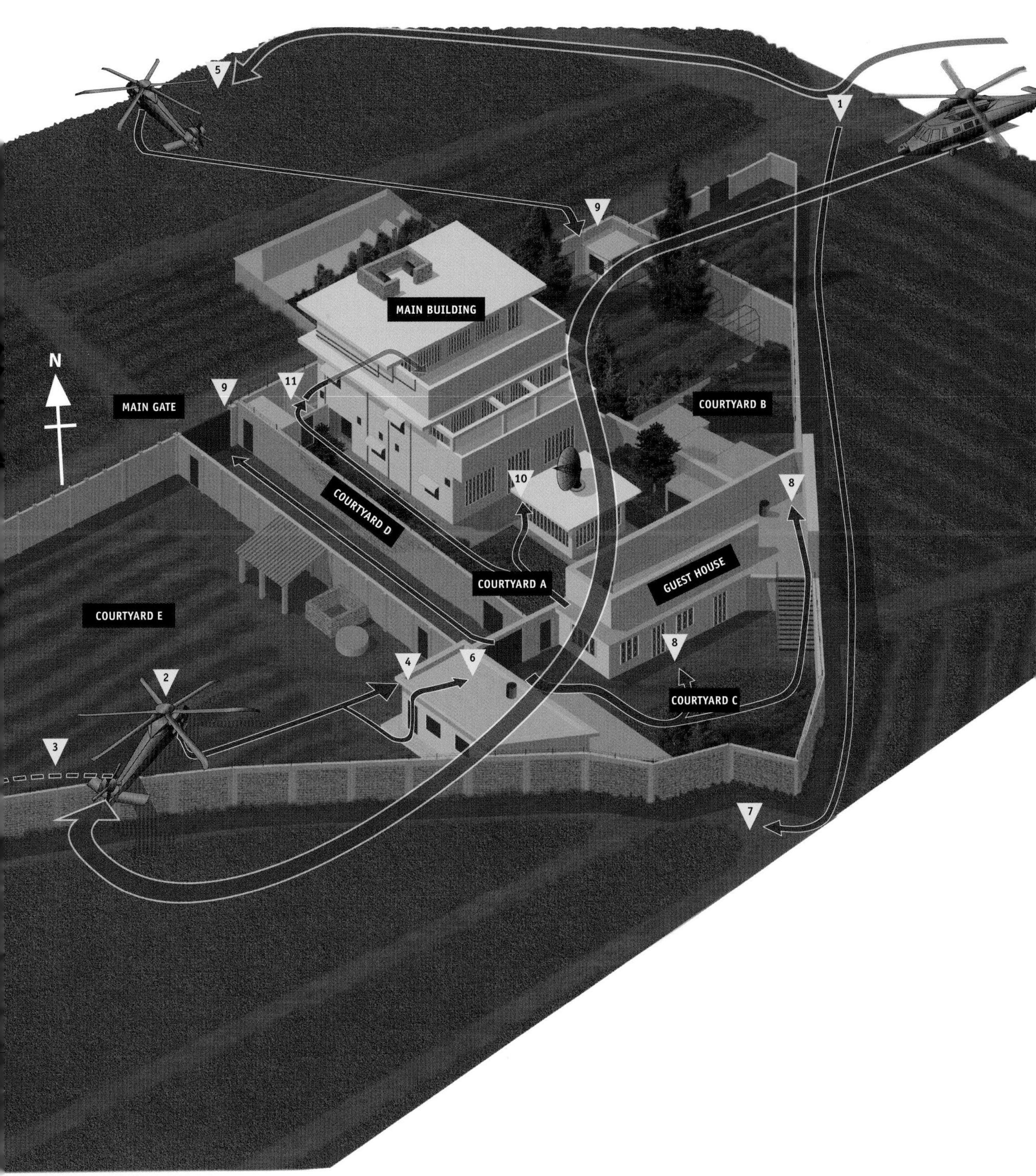
MAIN BUILDING
N
MAIN GATE
COURTYARD B
COURTYARD D
COURTYARD A
GUEST HOUSE
COURTYARD E
COURTYARD C
1
2
3
4
5
6
7
8
8
9
9
10
11

TACTICAL MISSION TIMELINE, OPERATION *NEPTUNE SPEAR* PHASE 3

All times are local Pakistani time.

0110 The SEAL team continues searching and clearing the compound.

0113 One QRF Chinook is dispatched to participate in the Exfil, to replace the crashed MH-X.

0114 SEALs make initial identification of bin Laden. SEAL Team Leader radios confirmation codeword "Geronimo" to Vice-Admiral William H. McCraven.

0115 SEALs seize and bag all computer hard drives, documents, DVDs, thumb-drives, and other "electronic equipment" for intelligence analysis, as well as weapons and a large stash of opium.

0116 The SEAL demo specialist places charges on crashed stealth helicopter for demolition.

0120 Two Pakistan Air Force F-16 Fighting Falcon jets are scrambled; this is reported immediately by US monitors.

0130 The QRF Chinook approaches to aid in the Exfil, but is waved off seconds before the demo is blown.

0135 The demolition charges on the crashed helicopter are blown. The QRF Chinook then lands outside of the compound.

0136 Sohaib Athar tweets: "A huge window shaking bang here in Abbottabad Cant [Cantonment]. I hope it's not the start of something nasty :-S"

0137 The Chinook and MH-X are uploaded and depart. The total time between Infil and Exfil is no more than 38 minutes.

0144 Sohaib Athar tweets: "all silent after the blast, but a friend heard it 6 km away too … the helicopter is gone too."

0200 The MH-X carrying bin Laden's body meets with the second Chinook at the refuel point, refuels and departs for the return flight to Afghanistan.

0230 CIA operatives abandon the Abbottabad "safe house" upon completion of *Neptune Spear*, and initiate egress.

0240 The MH-X and the two Chinooks cross safely back into Afghanistan airspace.

another as they had done on a hundred such missions. The SEAL assaulters still on the second floor heard both screaming and suppressed gunfire upstairs. They also saw reflected light from muzzle flashes above the stairwell. Several two-man teams immediately disengaged from clearing the second floor, and advanced up the stairs toward the third floor. The Chalk One leader was the first to arrive.

As the other SEALs began to enter bin Laden's bedroom, at least one of them fired shots into bin Laden's chest. Bin Laden's youngest wife, Amal was wounded in the leg, either from a bullet fragment or debris from the tile floor. She continued to scream. One of the SEALs related in a later interview in *Esquire* magazine that she came at him "like she wanted to fight me … or she wanted to die instead of him." The SEALs bound her with zip ties and put her on the bed with the other two women and bin Laden's three-year-old son. The rest of his children were kept outside the bedroom on the balcony.

Two SEALs cleared the remaining top floor rooms and confirmed to each other, "All clear over here." They radioed "Third deck secure" over the troop net and then added, "We got a possible jackpot." The combat assault portion of the raid was completed by 0112 hours, all within 15 minutes. They were then safe to flip up their night vision devices and turn on their helmet-mounted Maglites to try to identify bin Laden. The body lay on the bedroom carpet between the foot of the bed and the doorway. The fatal head-wounds were ghastly, with the upper left side of his forehead severed and split down to his eye socket.

Identifying the body

As others came in to see him. One SEAL referred to as "Tom" said, "I think this is our boy." However, it was an educated guess. Owen later related, "No one was sure. It could have been anybody." His face had to be cleaned off before even an initial identification could be made, or photos taken. Part of the sub-tasks were to take clear photos of the whole of each target's face, and transmit them immediately. The SEAL practice, according to the SEAL interviewed in *Esquire*, was, "If you kill him, then you clean him." But, the person who purportedly shot bin Laden was somewhat caught up in the moment, and deferred to a fellow SEAL who stepped in. Owen told him, "Walt and I will run with this," and took out his own camera. Tom left the room and reported over the command net, "We have a possible, I repeat *possible* touchdown on the third deck."

Owen and "Walt" donned rubber gloves and went to work. After wiping away the blood, they began to see some resemblance to bin Laden. Walt took out his DNA kit and began to take several samples of blood, saliva and bone marrow. This was all required in case, for any reason, they could not get the body back into US custody for definitive DNA identification. Owen asked Walt to help him hold bin Laden's remaining "good eye" open for a photo. When Walt had difficulty extracting bone marrow from his thigh with the spring-injected syringe, Owen handed over his own syringe and said, "Here. Try this one." This was reportedly how bone marrow DNA samples of bin Laden were left behind for the Pakistanis. (A set of one SEAL's color "Target Identification" cards were also left behind for the Pakistanis to recover.)

Meanwhile, a SEAL called "Will" treated the leg wound of Amal Ahmed Abdul Fatah, the crying youngest wife of Osama bin Laden. It was a small wound and she finally stopped making so much noise. As a self-taught Arabic speaker, he tried to confirm the dead man's identity with her. He asked Amal, "The dead Sheikh – what is his name?" But she only provided several aliases. Having dealt with similar situations many times in Afghanistan, Will knew to ask the children.

MAY 2, 0109 HOURS

Osama bin Laden is shot dead in his third-floor hideout

"Khalid? Khalid?" (overleaf)

This scene depicts another crucial point in the mission at approximately 0108 hours. SEAL assaulters have advanced to the main building's second floor and secured the hallway in all directions while other two-man teams clear inside the media rooms. The point man encounters bin Laden's 23-year-old son Khalid armed with an AK-47 assault rifle in the 3rd-floor stairwell. The "green glow" is the view that an operator experiences when peering through his helmet-mounted GPNVG-18 "Quadeye" panoramic night vision goggles (NVGs) into the pitch-black darkness. While covering the stairwell, the point man saw and heard movement on the upper flight of stairs. Based on pre-mission intelligence, he whispered out in the dark, "Khalid? Khalid?"

Khalid poked his head around the corner of the stairwell and looked into the darkness. The point man aimed his weapon and laser pointer and fired one shot into Khalid bin Laden's chin. The bullet traveled up into his skull and killed him instantly. His body dropped onto the landing. Other SEAL assaulters "double-tapped" him in the chest as they advanced up the stairs to find Osama bin Laden on the third floor.

The SEALs selected a configuration of infrared laser pointers to mount on their weapons to produce a beam and aiming-point dot that are invisible to the naked eye. The beam can only be seen through the SEAL's NVGs. Each SEAL also personalized his own equipment configuration, with body armor in varied configurations with pouch and flex-cuffs and other equipment attached. Note also, that in *Neptune Spear* SEAL uniforms had built-in pockets for kneepads and no external padding as seen on older uniforms.

SHUMATE
2013

US President Barack Obama and Vice President Joe Biden, along with members of the national security team, receive an update on Operation *Neptune Spear* in one of the conference rooms of the Situation Room of the White House, May 1, 2011. They are watching a live feed from drones operating over the bin Laden complex. (Pete Souza/US Government)

He went outside onto the balcony and asked, "Who is this man?" One of the little girls did not know to lie about his name. She responded "Osama." Will asked again, smiling at the girl. "Osama? Osama who?" The girl responded, "Osama bin Laden."

"Are you sure that is Osama bin Laden?" Will insisted. The girl responded with a clear "Yes." Will then came back into the hallway and grabbed one of the other two wives by her arms, giving her a good shake. "Who is the man in the bedroom?" She stated that it was Osama bin Laden. Will reported this to Tom with the words, "Hey, dual confirmation! I confirmed it with the kid. Confirmed it with the old lady. Both are saying the same thing."

The SEALs called for the mission commander officer, who came upstairs. Tom reported to him that the girl and one of the wives had confirmed it was bin Laden. He looked at the body and said, "Yeah, that looks like our guy." After this confirmation the mission commander "Red 02" stepped outside and used a satellite phone to call Vice-Admiral McRaven. He sent the prescribed code words for the primary mission objective: "Geronimo. Geronimo. Geronimo." He added, "For God and country, I pass Geronimo." When asked whether bin Laden's status was killed or captured, he responded, "Geronimo EKIA." (enemy killed in action).

Owen transmitted his photos back for further identification. While photographing the body he noticed two weapons on a shelf by the bedroom door: a Russian-made Kalashnikov AKSU-74 and a Makarov pistol. Both weapons were unloaded. In all, three AK-47s and two pistols were reported as recovered; all were used or prepared for use, except those in bin Laden's room. Owen's view was that bin Laden "had no intention of fighting." Owen allegedly also found a bottle of *Just for Men* beard dye in bin Laden's room.

One of the assaulters on the second floor found the computers and files in the media rooms and called over the troop net, "Hey, we have a significant amount of SSE [sensitive site exploitation] on the second deck. We are going to need any extra [SEALs] down here." As the process of identifying bin Laden continued on the third floor, the remaining team members conducted a thorough search of every room and closet of the main building and the rest of the compound. They cleared barricades, including a false door, gathered weapons stashes and placed all of the women and children in one location, treating minor wounds on some.

In the second floor media rooms several SEALs were busy breaking open the computers and removing the hard drives. They collected all of the thumb drives, CDs, DVDs, VHS tapes and cameras into their net collection bags carried for this purpose. Under the single beds in the computer rooms they found large duffel bags stuffed full of raw opium in vacuum-sealed plastic bags.

During the SSE, the SEALs in Chalk Two became aware for the first time that Chalk One's stealth helicopter had crash landed in the courtyard. One team leader stated, "We're never getting out of here now," adding that he did not want to "have to steal cars and drive to Islamabad [US Embassy location]".

However, the primary contingency of bringing up the QRF was still available. After the commander was informed that the helicopter was not flyable, he reported this to higher command. Vice-Admiral McRaven immediately gave orders for the QRF Chinook to come forward from the FARP. McRaven then reported up his chain of command: "We will now be amending the mission. We have a helicopter down in the courtyard. My men are prepared for this contingency, and they will deal with it." By 0113 hours, Romeo-2, the QRF Chinook, was dispatched to fly from the FARP to conduct the "Exfil", and replace the crashed MH-X.

Chief Mike called over the troop net to destroy the damaged MH-X with the words, "Demo team, prep it to blow." The SEAL in charge of demo told the EOD (explosive ordnance) tech: "Hey! We're going to blow it now!" The tech responded affirmitively and began to implement the contingency plan to demo the entire main building. When he began placing C4 charges and detonators around the first floor of the main building, the SEAL grabbed him, asking, "What in the [expletive] are you doing?" The tech replied, "You told me to get ready to blow it, right?" "Not the house," the SEAL said. "The helo!" The EOD responded, "What helo?" The confusion was soon cleared up.

The "Exfil"

By 0116 the EOD tech was busy placing charges onto the crashed MH-X for demolition, while the other MH-X, call sign Prince 52, was circling nearby, waiting for word to return. Fuel was running low, and time was limited. With the damaged helicopter unable to fly, the pilots and crew chief were instructed to destroy all classified equipment, and then blow up the aircraft to prevent compromise of its classified stealth capability. They began to smash the flight and communications devices in the cockpit, just in case anything was blown clear in the explosion.

INSIDE THE MAIN BUILDING

MAY 2, 2011

EVENTS

1 Three SEALs enter building by south door and kill Abrar and Bushra in first floor room. The SEALs clear the floor

2 Four SEALs enter by north door

3 These SEALs break open stair gate and climb to second floor

4 SEALs clear the second floor

5 Climbing to third floor, the point man shoots Khalid bin Laden halfway up the stairs

6 As point man reaches third floor, he shoots Osama bin Laden in the bedroom

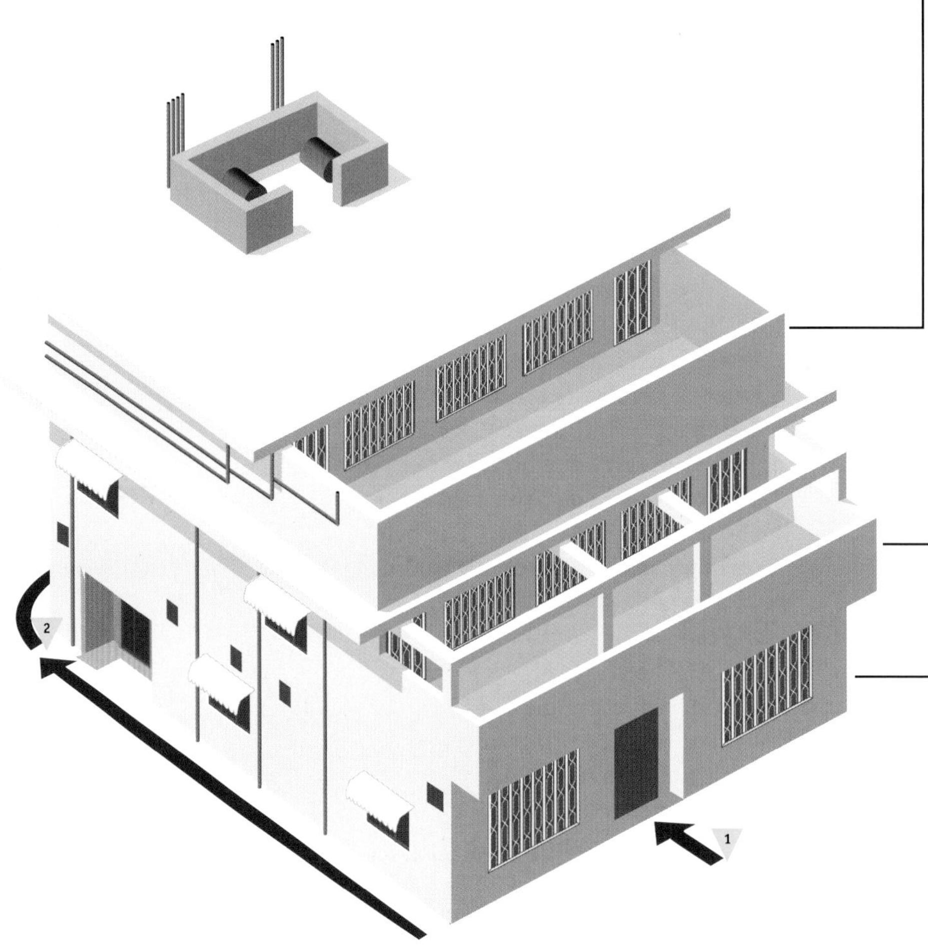

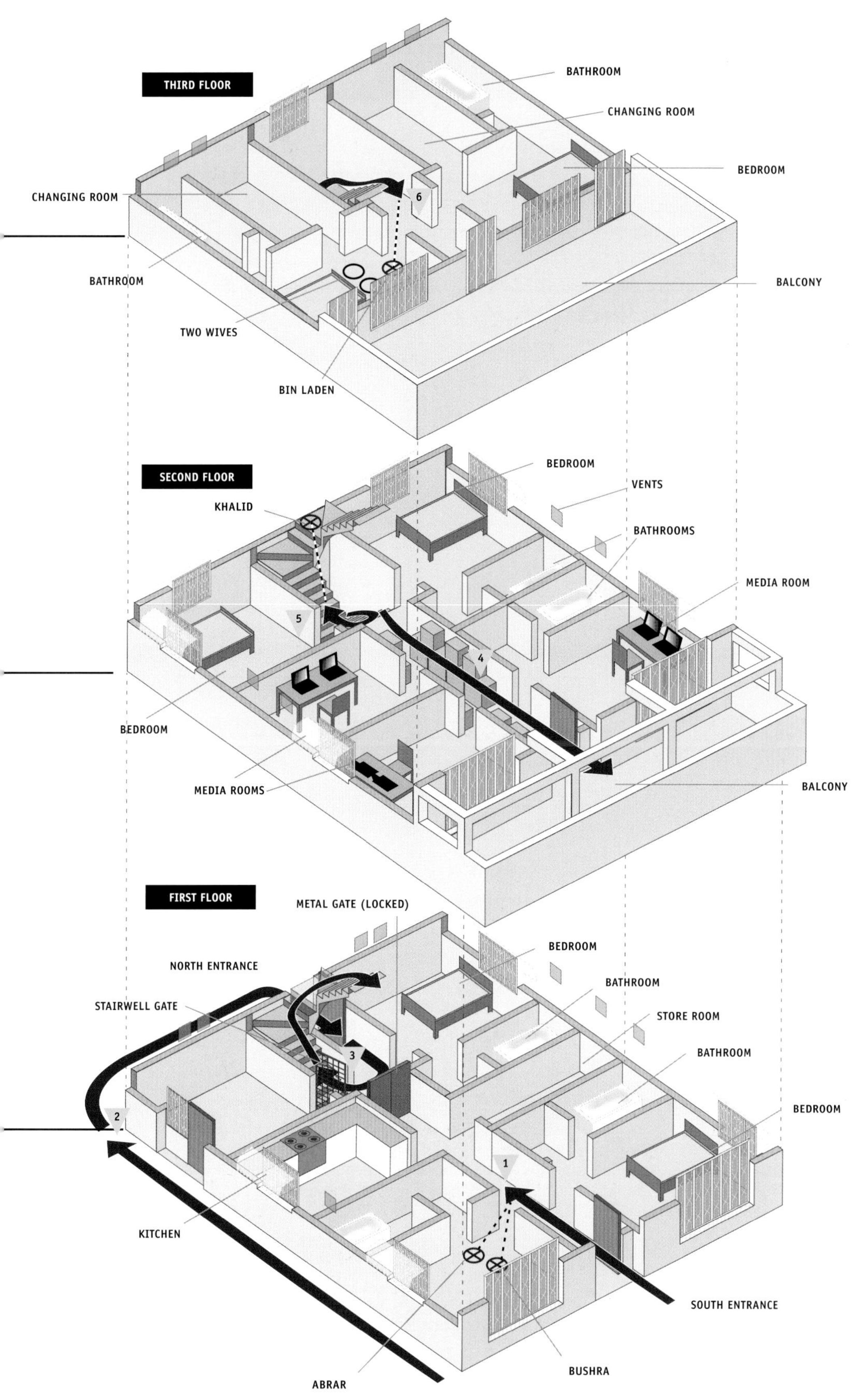
THIRD FLOOR
BATHROOM
CHANGING ROOM
BEDROOM
CHANGING ROOM
6
BATHROOM
BALCONY
TWO WIVES
BIN LADEN
SECOND FLOOR
BEDROOM
VENTS
KHALID
BATHROOMS
MEDIA ROOM
5
4
BEDROOM
MEDIA ROOMS
BALCONY
FIRST FLOOR
METAL GATE (LOCKED)
BEDROOM
NORTH ENTRANCE
BATHROOM
STAIRWELL GATE
STORE ROOM
3
BATHROOM
BEDROOM
2
1
KITCHEN
SOUTH ENTRANCE
BUSHRA
ABRAR

Chief Mike called out "time hacks" to the SEAL team on the radio. At 0125 he radioed "Ten minutes," and soon after the power and the lights came back on. Several of them zipped bin Laden's corpse into a body bag and dragged him down the stairs and out into the courtyard by the front gate.

The security perimeter team came over the radio reporting a local Pakistani presence. Outside of the walls, they could be heard warning off Pakistani onlookers, ordering in Pashto, "Go back inside! There is a security operation under way!" No Pakistani police had arrived yet. Above them, their UAV support was providing localized jamming of Pakistani military and police communications (along with surveillance and network relay capabilities.)

The senior SEAL in the main building media room radioed, "We need ten more minutes. We're not even halfway done." They had bagged a lot of materials, but were still finding more documents and electronic data for intelligence analysis. Chief Mike finally said, "Post assault, five minutes." They had to upload and depart fast or the aircraft would run out of fuel. He broadcast an urgent call to all, "Hey guys! Drop what you're doing NOW and move to EXFIL HLZ."

As demolition of the downed stealth helicopter was imminent, Chief Mike transmitted to all, "Consolidate the women and children and get them out of the compound." Instead of following these instructions, and with time running short, Owen led al-Kuwaiti's family over into the concrete guesthouse where the other woman and children were. He motioned to them and ordered in English, "Stay here!" Other SEALs reportedly moved other surviving residents into the guesthouse before the explosion. The bodies of the other three men and one woman killed during the raid were left where they lay for Pakistani forces to recover.

Chalk One was designated to go on the Prince 52 MH-X with the body, as it was a smaller, more maneuverable aircraft. The surviving helicopter flew in and landed on top of a strobe light the SEALs had placed in a field across from the compound's main gate. Owen and three SEALs carried the body bag to the MH-X and climbed in. They waited a few minutes while the pilots tried to be sure they had a visual of the arriving Chinook before lifting up.

The remaining SEALs and Prince 51's aircrew piled up the SSE materials near the gate, waiting for the QRF Chinook. They heard the rotors approaching and heard a radio call saying, "We are 30 seconds out." Soon after this, the demo tech ran out calling to the Commander, "Call off the 47! You need to get all of the birds out of the area. The charge is going to go off in under 30 seconds." He had already set the timers on the charges.

On board the MH-X, SEAL Tom shouted, "Let's go! We have to take off right now!" To avoid being hit by explosion debris the helicopter took off immediately and left the vicinity. The commander then waved off the Chinook only seconds before it flew over. One SEAL reported that it was "almost blown out of the sky" by their own explosive charges. The Chinook flew away from the compound and made a wide circle around Abbottabad.

Those SEALs still on the ground took cover behind the compound walls as the charges detonated at approximately 0135. Bin Laden's wife Amal had continued to scream insults at them in Arabic. After the helicopter explosives detonated inside the compound, nothing further was heard from her.

After the explosion, the Chinook circled around and landed outside the compound. A tall and bright flame from the burning MH-X's fuel now illuminated the night. The SEALs quickly uploaded and the Chinook departed at about 0138. The total time between Infil and Exfil was no more than 38 minutes.

By 0144 all had fallen silent. After it was confirmed that both aircraft had made it safely away from the city, local operatives, vehicles and private security contractors in the Abbottabad area were released. Other operatives in Abbottabad abandoned their safe house and initiated egress from the area.

The Chinook followed the planned route back towards Afghanistan. The stealth helicopter, however, was critically low on fuel, and so headed for the FARP at Kandar (Hassanzai). Inside the cramped MH-X, one SEAL sat on bin Laden's body bag.

Given the amount of noise and attention they had generated, and flying away from the city in a large, slow-moving Chinook, many of the assault team felt this was one of the most vulnerable times for the entire mission. However, given that it was dark and that they were overflying mountainous terrain, the Pakistani air defense systems and intercept fighters could not easily detect the helicopters. With extensive US electronic warfare assets able to monitor, false-feed and jam all enemy radar, navigational, command control and communications functions, none of the circling US combat aircraft would be required to respond or cross the Pakistani border.

By 0205 local time, the MH-X with bin Laden's body had landed at the FARP at Kandar (Hassanzai). Several SEALs dismounted the aircraft to secure the area while the specialist went to work. While sitting at the refuel

After the raid, Pakistani boys collect debris at the site of the crashed MH-X helicopter outside the compound. The villa that hid bin Laden from the world was put under Pakistani police control, as the world's media sought to catch glimpses of the debris left by the US raid that killed him. (Aamir Qureshi/AFP/Getty Images)

THE EXFIL

MAY 2, 2011

EVENTS

1 SEALs transfer SSE material and body-bag containing bin Laden to outside the compound, as demolition charges are set on the crashed MH-X

2 Chalk One SEALs board surviving MH-X with bin Laden body-bag, and lift off prior to detonation and Chinook's arrival

3 Surviving women and children are secured in the Guest House during demo of crashed aircraft and Exfil

4 Demolition charges on crashed MH-X are detonated causing a large explosion, fireball and debris. The helicopter's fuel continues to burn into the night

5 QRF Chinook turns and circles to narrowly avoid explosion and debris from MH-X demolition

6 QRF Chinook lands to upload all remaining SEALs and SSE material. Chinook lifts off to return directly to Jalalabad SOF base

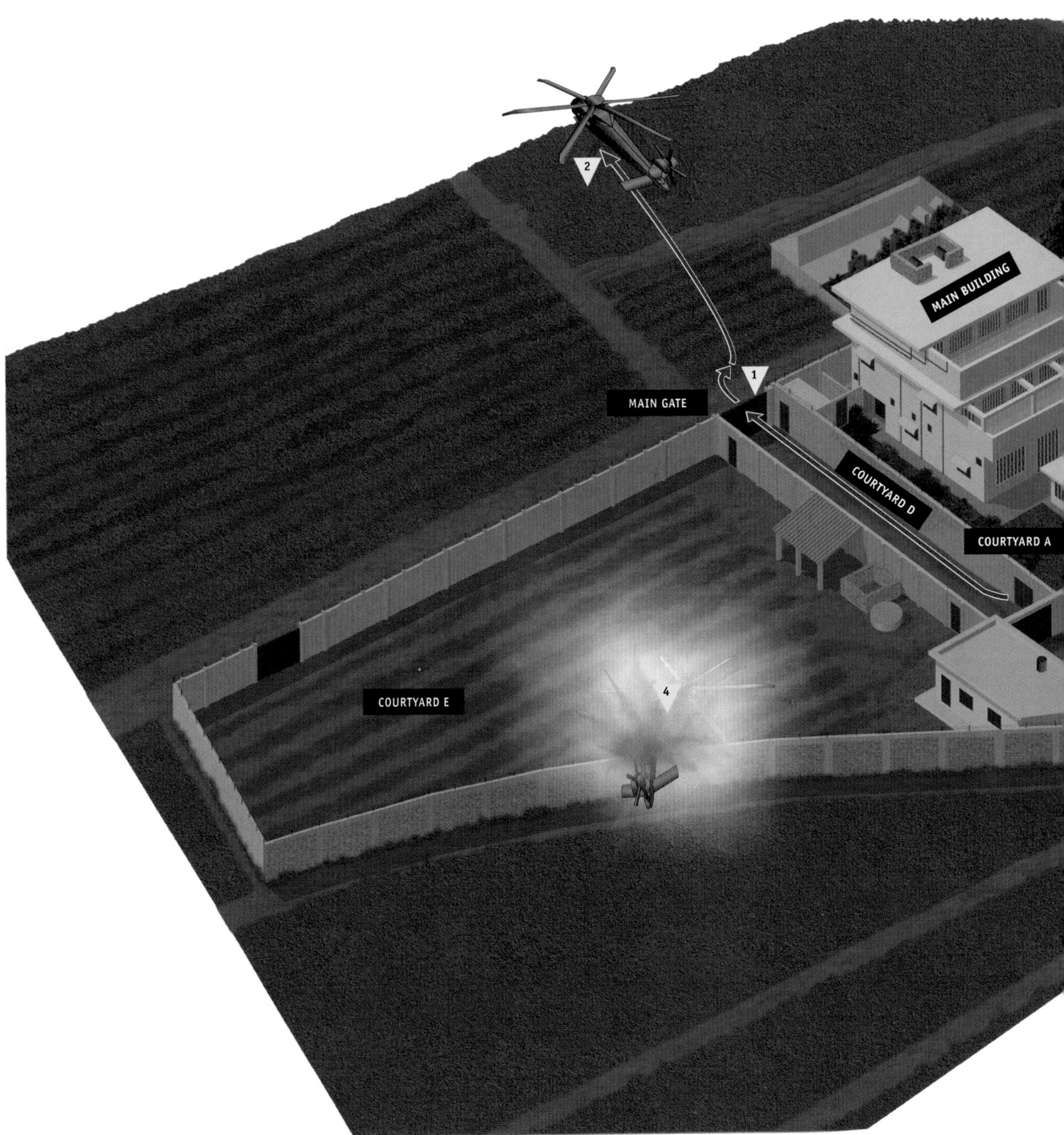

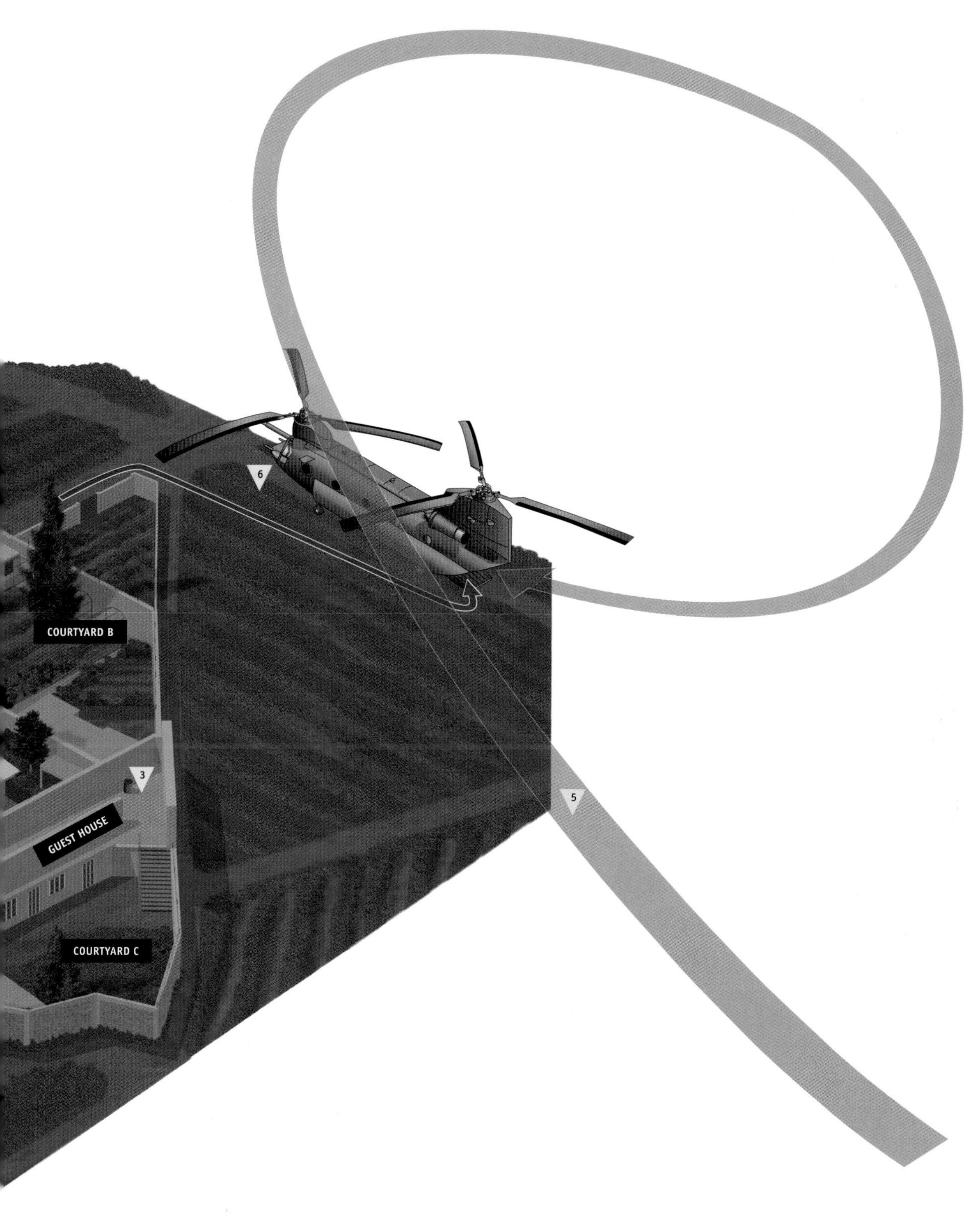
6
COURTYARD B
3
GUEST HOUSE
5
COURTYARD C

point Tom notified the helicopter's occupants over the intercom, "To save on weight, they want four or five of us to get off and ride back with the 47." So, five SEALs got off and walked over to board the refueler Chinook.

By 0207, the Pakistani chief of air staff had been notified of an operation and unidentified aircraft over their military facility in Abbottabad, and that it was clear the aircraft did not belong to Pakistan. He gave the order to scramble their Air Defense Alert fighter aircraft with "clear instructions to shoot down any aircraft or helicopter flying over Abbottabad, or in the adjoining area" (*Abbottabad Commission Report*, p. 144). The FARP at Kandar was in the adjoining area.

Two Pakistan Air Force F-16 Fighting Falcon jets were alerted and prepared for take-off from PAF Base Mushaf located in Sargodha, Punjab Province, about 200 miles south of Abbottabad. Once the jets were airborne, flight time would be less than 15 minutes. The US monitors and surveillance measures were aware of the order, and would detect their take-off immediately. A response by US combat aircraft was available, but not yet needed.

It took about 20 minutes to refuel the near-empty MH-X. Once completed, the captured local farmer Abdul Munaf was released, and both aircraft took off for their return flight back to Afghanistan. Once airborne, SEAL Tom made a suggestion: "Let's search the body again and make sure we didn't miss anything." Bin Laden was wearing the *kurta pajama,* a loose-fitting tunic and pants; an emergency fund of 500 Euros was found sewn into the fabric of his pants, together with two phone numbers of a pre-arranged local contact to aid in any escape.

At 0339 local time, Sohaib Athar tweeted that jets were flying over Abbottabad. The helicopters, continuing to avoid detection, again flew NOE (nap-of-the-earth) through valleys and behind screening mountain ranges. After almost an hour, with increased dispersion between them, the stealth helicopter and both Chinooks crossed safely back into Afghanistan airspace. One of the crew chiefs on the trail Chinook announced on the intercom, "You probably thought you'd never hear this, but welcome home to Afghanistan." After another 15 minutes they saw the lights of Jalalabad, and landed.

AFTERMATH

Operation *Neptune Spear* had been successfully completed with no casualties, and the entire assault force returned to Jalalabad with the SSE material and the body of Osama bin Laden at 0255 AFT on May 2, 2011. It had taken just under three hours and 40 minutes. The returning aircraft set down on the JSOC helipad, where a ring of bright lights faced outward to obscure the view in all directions. The pilots began flicking switches and calling out their checks. The aircraft engines shut down and the whirring rotors slowed, all of which mechanically echoed everyone's sigh of relief.

Each participant initiated his post mission routines with their habitual professionalism. All confirmed that their "sensitive items" (weapons, communications, NVGs and classified items) were secure, and leaders re-accounted for and rechecked the physical condition of each of their people. Those on the Chinooks piled their equipment and bags of SSE material at the end of the ramps. The Chalk One SEALs, who had custody of bin Laden's body bag, began to clamber out of their MH-X helicopter. Three soldiers in highly distinguishable US Army Ranger apparel approached them from a pickup parked on the tarmac. The Rangers had been assigned the task of carrying bin Laden's body from Jalalabad to Bagram Air Base, Afghanistan. One of the SEALs waved them off with, "No! We got this!" – they were going to retain custody of their prize. The SEALs carried the body bag to the pickup truck and rode with it over to the hangar.

Vice-Admiral William McRaven was in front of the hangar wearing his desert digital-camouflage Special Ops uniform. He was apparently eager to see the body. He told the SEALs, "Let's see him." They dropped the bag off the tailgate and Owen unzipped it, saying, "There's your boy!" Owen pulled the beard and tilted the head from side to side and added, "He obviously just dyed his beard. He doesn't look as old as I expected." Inside the bag in a pool of congealed blood, his face gray and partially disfigured from the gunshot wounds, bin Laden appeared small.

MAY 2, 0255 HOURS

Assault force returns to Jalalabad with the body of Osama bin Laden

President Barack Obama shakes hands with Admiral Mike Mullen, CJCS, in the Green Room of the White House following his statement detailing the operation against Osama bin Laden. CIA Director Leon Panetta and Secretary of State Hillary Clinton are pictured at left. (Pete Souza/ US Government)

Vice-Admiral McRaven knelt beside him to look more closely, as more of the men crowded around to see their target. Most of the participants had not yet paused from their duties to look at him. McRaven then said, "He is supposed to be 6 feet, 4 inches tall." He had a SEAL of that height lie adjacent to the body. The height was the same. It was at this point that multiple other gunshot wounds to the chest and legs were evident. These were redundant, as the first two were obviously fatal. One of the QRF SEALs asked, "Hey who shot him?" One of the SEALs, who came to be known as "the shooter," claimed responsibility.

Shortly after, JSOC officers took the shooter and point man aside for a "shooters-only debrief." "Jen," the female CIA analyst who was primarily responsible for doggedly tracking down bin Laden, was appropriately present. She expressed no desire to see his body, but she was persuaded to look and give identification. "Is that your guy?" the shooter asked her, as he gave her a memento of the magazine from the weapon used to kill him. It was clearly an emotional moment for all. Owen walked over and hugged the MH-X helicopter pilot and thanked him for saving their lives. Without his skilled piloting, he asserted, "we all would have been in a pile of debris in the courtyard."

With the equipment and SSE material offloaded and sorted, the operation's entire personnel went to work gathering and transferring all the materials, bin Laden's body and all personnel onto two USAF C-130 Hercules transport aircraft, which were waiting to ferry everything and everyone to Bagram Air Base for further processing. Reverting back into routine mode, most of the SEALs slept during the 45-minute trip.

At Bagram everything was once again offloaded and turned in. The SEALs were given breakfast and were able to relax somewhat before JSOC officers conducted a full debriefing and after action review (AAR) to record and analyze what had transpired. The leaders stayed beyond this for further review. The pilots participated in a USAF AAR and, again, the point man and the shooter were called over to another longer "shooters-only" debrief session.

The Pakistani media began to broadcast reports of unidentified aircraft crashing in Abbottabad. With news of multiple explosions, a burning helicopter, gunfire, four dead bodies, and bin Laden's relatives left behind, it was only a matter of time before the story broke in the Pakistani military and government. To sway Pakistani speculation, Admiral Mike Mullen, Chairman of the Joint Chiefs of Staff, was directed to call his Pakistani counterpart, General Ashfaq Parvez Kayani and to advise him personally of the operation.

At 0500 Osama bin Laden's body was flown in a V-22 Osprey, escorted by two F/A-18 fighters, to the aircraft carrier USS *Carl Vinson* afloat in the northern Arabian Sea. Once DNA evidence had confirmed beyond doubt that the dead body was that of Osama bin Laden, he was buried at sea.

Back in Abbottabad, local police had taken control of the compound by sunrise, and were keeping away onlookers. They took custody of all of the surviving women and children as well as the four bodies of Khalid bin Laden, Ahmed al-Kuwaiti, Abrar al-Kuwaiti, and Abrar's wife Bushra. Later the QRF from the Military Cantonment arrived to cordon off the area. By 0800 hours Pakistani investigators were searching door to door in the Abbottabad compound to gather information and ensure no other persons had escaped and were hiding locally. The Pakistan ISI reported later that the total number of people in the compound at the time of the raid was 17. Interestingly, a conflicting ISI report noted that one female told Pakistani investigators that one of bin Laden's sons was taken away, and that bin Laden had been captured alive, and then shot dead in front of family members before being dragged to a helicopter. No other corroboration of this claim has come to light.

AFTERMATH TIMELINE

Unless otherwise stated, times are AFT.

0255 Operation *Neptune Spear* team arrives at Jalalabad, Afghanistan with body of Osama bin Laden and captured intelligence.

0300 Chairman of the Joint Chiefs of Staff (CJCS) Admiral Mike Mullen calls Pakistan's army chief General Ashfaq Parvez Kayani to advise him of the raid.

0325 SEALs and bin Laden's body are flown to Bagram Air Base, Afghanistan for further identification.

0500 Osama bin Laden's body is flown in a V-22 Osprey – escorted by two US Navy F/A-18 fighter jets – to the aircraft carrier USS *Carl Vinson* in the northern Arabian Sea.

2300 EDT DNA cross-checking confirms that the dead body was that of bin Laden.

1100 (local time) Bin Laden's burial at sea is completed.

2335 EDT President Obama appears on US television networks from the White House and announces that Osama bin Laden has been killed.

ANALYSIS

Operation *Neptune Spear* is considered by many as one of the most exemplary special operations case histories in the annals of special operations warfare. It is fitting that Vice-Admiral William H. McRaven's own special operations models and principles, as well as his concept of relative superiority, examined in his own book *Spec Ops: Case Studies in Special Operations Warfare – Theory and Practice*, would be appropriate for evaluating the mission.

Relative superiority and the Spec Ops model

Vice-Admiral McRaven's Spec Ops doctrine stipulates that the concept of relative superiority is "crucial to the theory of [successful] Special Operations." He defines relative superiority in *Spec Ops* as a condition attained when an attacking special operations force reaches the point of achieving a decisive advantage, and the enemy has no defensive advantage.

The question thus raised is, when and how – in his plan for Operation *Neptune Spear* – did Vice-Admiral McRaven project his SEALs would achieve the state of relative superiority over the compound defenders? Moreover, when and how – in the actual execution of Operation *Neptune Spear* – did the SEALs achieve the state of relative superiority and guarantee success?

We find the answer to the first question in Vice-Admiral McRaven's guidance on inserting the assaulters: "The most important thing is to get them on the ground safe, and they'll figure out the rest." This indicates that he identified the point of attaining relative superiority as after the assaulters were inserted onto the ground inside or outside of the compound. This is a logical conclusion. As long as the SEALs were aboard the two stealth helicopters, only two hits at close range (or one hit and a subsequent collision) would be needed to cause the operation to crash catastrophically. Once both rotorcraft had inserted all of their assaulters, the overwhelming numbers, lethal technological superiority and skill as trained killers would

On May 3, 2011, Osama bin Laden's name was removed from the FBI's Ten Most Wanted list. He had been on the list since 1999, following the bombings of the US Embassies in Dar es Salaam, Tanzania and Nairobi, Kenya. (FBI)

make killing bin Laden pretty much a foregone conclusion. The events proved Vice-Admiral McRaven right in that assumption.

However, to answer the second question, it is only now apparent that bin Laden had placed all of his personal security focus into the exertion of tradecraft secrecy and simply "never being found," as opposed to into preparing for violent resistance. At the time of the raid, however, no one could predict whether or not anti-aircraft missiles, RPGs, suicide vests, hand grenades, booby-traps, or wiring the entire compound with explosives were planned for use. The presence of children, many of them bin Laden's own would seem to mitigate that, but not conclusively. With only a few of the right tools in hand, and the same willingness to resist as was demonstrated, the raid very well could have degenerated into a very bloody mess for all parties.

All in all, the only hitch in the mission was the crash of the MH-X call sign Prince 51 and the failure during training to rehearse "realistically" by employing the stealth helicopters over concrete walls (instead of the chain-link fences used). However, the skills and experience of the Prince 51 pilot saved the men on board (if not the aircraft) from being lost. The skill and experience of the SEAL assaulters enabled them to carry on the mission without hesitation, and the forfeiture of surprise did not help bin Laden or any of the armed defenders to survive, or even to take anyone with them.

Operation *Neptune Spear* was "a simple plan, carefully concealed, repeatedly and realistically rehearsed and executed with surprise, speed and purpose." All six principles were amply demonstrated. The mission clearly limited the number of objectives to two: kill or capture Osama bin Laden, and return with his body for final positive identification and disposal; and conduct SSE to recover all possible documents, electronic data, hardware and materials for intelligence evaluation. Both were successfully achieved. The mission also clearly had very good intelligence and used overwhelming technological and tactical innovation. Security was so effective that bin Laden and the Pakistani authorities were never tipped off, and were surprised. The team had rehearsed their assault so comprehensively in a realistic mock-up of the compound that the loss of a helicopter did not hinder them at all. They successfully completed both primary objectives very rapidly and well within the time constraints necessary with no casualties other than the loss of one valuable aircraft.

Good intelligence and innovation

The plan for Operation *Neptune Spear* relied heavily on accurate intelligence. The many months of intensive, multi-platform surveillance failed to confirm bin Laden's presence. However, it did provide JSOC planners with an extensive quantity of detailed information about the compound, all of the occupants and all potential threats.

William H. McRaven asserts that "good intelligence" is a critical element because it reduces costly surprises or "unknown factors" that can seriously complicate an operation and result in disaster. For *Neptune Spear*, the intelligence was both extensive and accurate. As a result, there were very few surprises.

A critical factor in the operation's success was the continuation of the CIA's extensive long-term surveillance and intelligence gathering efforts, all of which had made the raid possible. This would include multiple methods of continuous aerial, satellite and on-the-ground surveillance, as well as electronic intelligence collection and in-depth monitoring of the activity and communications of the Pakistani police and military forces, the country's air defense and radar networks, and the PAF during the mission.

Neptune Spear planners also sought to use innovative methods, such as the effective use of technology and the employment of unconventional or unexpected tactics. In McRaven's words, "Innovation simplifies a plan by helping to avoid or eliminate obstacles that would otherwise compromise, surprise and/or complicate the rapid execution of the mission." Such obstacles were numerous in *Neptune Spear*. The primary complication was the need to insert an assault team into an interior city in Pakistan, complete a combat mission in close proximity to a Pakistani military base and then return to Afghanistan without detection or interception by the Pakistani military and the Pakistani Air Force.

The most obvious and effective innovation used to reduce the risk of Pakistani detection during the mission was a technological one – the first operational use of the MH-X stealth helicopter. The MH-X was not only quiet enough to retain the element of surprise upon approach to the objective, but also had radar-invisible qualities to prevent detection by the Pakistani military. The use of surveillance and munitions-capable drones deployed to support the mission was a further innovative aspect.

The unknown aspect that most threatened the success of the mission related to the interior of the objective itself. It was impossible to gather detailed intelligence on what was inside the compound's multiple buildings without compromising the mission. The existence or absence of modifications to the building, physical obstructions, underground bunkers, wired explosives, false walls, escape tunnels, hidden compartments or other defenses were all unknown. The same applied to the occupants' weapons,

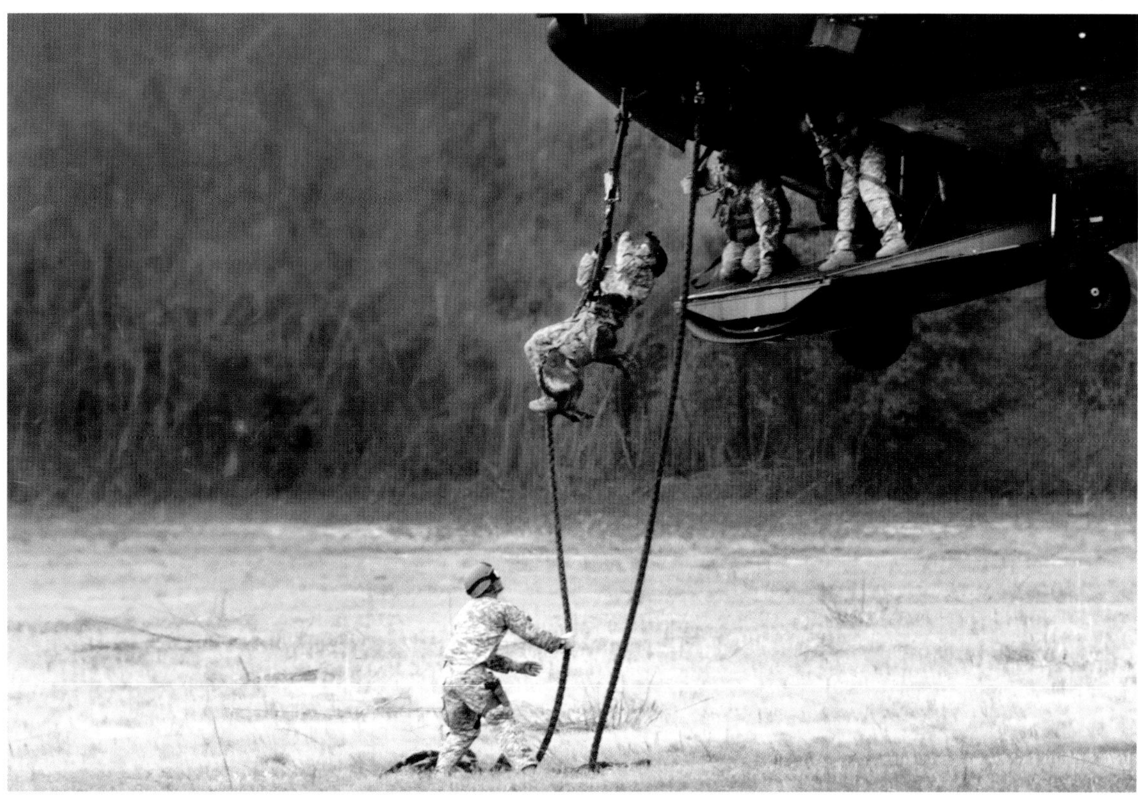

small arms, anti-aircraft armaments, and/or explosive suicide-vests. The planners had to assume the worst and prepare to advance into a strange, confusing and hostile environment against an armed enemy.

The mission planners chose to use stealth and surprise to mitigate as much of this as possible, namely approaching on a moonless night, using stealth aircraft, and fast-roping into the compound and onto the third-floor roof of the main building. The latter not only ensured quick access to the third floor via the balcony, but the rapid and stealthy deployment of SEALs onto the roof could also reduce or eliminate the threat of missile, rocket or small-arms anti-aircraft fire from the roof.

One low-tech innovation employed during *Neptune Spear* was the veteran SEAL combat assault dog Cairo, a Belgian Malinois, to support the mission. Fast-roping from a helicopter (here a Chinook, in an exercise) with a military working dog requires the animal to be harnessed to the soldier with custom equipment. Belgian Malinois are lighter than the traditional German Shepherd breed, and are generally used for fast-roping or parachute deployment. (Senior Airman Staci Miller/US Air Force)

One unconventional tactic employed was to "turn out the lights" on the objective. Operatives in Abbottabad (most likely Pakistani private security contractors) had arranged for a power blackout in the area to occur precisely during the time of the mission. Since rolling power blackouts are not uncommon there, this would not raise much suspicion. Several blackouts in the weeks before the mission also helped support that premise. With no power or lighting, the objective would be pitch-black inside and outside and the occupants (if they had no night vision devices) would be totally blinded. The assaulters, with state-of-the art night vision goggles, would hold an overwhelming advantage by being able to see through the darkness against a blind enemy. The assaulters could also acquire targets with exceptional precision using infrared laser pointers on each weapon. The laser pointers provided an added safety factor in avoiding potential friendly fire by

IN THE WAKE OF *NEPTUNE SPEAR*

May 6, 2011 al-Qaeda confirms bin Laden's death.

June 3 The al-Qaeda military commander and strategist Ilyas Kashmiri is killed by a Predator drone strike in southern Waziristan.

August 1 Media sources report that the Pakistani authorities have permitted Chinese scientists to analyze the US stealth helicopter's tail section and radar-absorbing paint. The claims are denied by Pakistan and China.

August 6 A CH-47 Chinook is shot down by RPG fire in Afghanistan killing 38, including 25 US Navy SEALs from SEAL Team Six and 5 members of 160th SOAR.

February 2012 The Pakistani authorities demolish bin Laden's compound in Abbottabad.

December 23, 2012 Commander John W. Price, SEAL Team Four commander in Afghanistan, is found dead from apparent suicide.

showing where every friendly weapon was pointed. In addition, all weapons were equipped with silencers. This enabled assaulters to fire quietly without giving away their positions or drawing added attention from the Pakistanis; it also ensured that assaulters could immediately identify any shots fired by the occupants as "hostile fire."

Other principles of Vice-Admiral McRaven's special operations model are inherent in the overall plan as it was developed. Under extremely tight security, the notice that Osama bin Laden was the ultimate target was kept from all but those who had a valid need to know; moreover, none were informed before they needed to know. Many contributing participants were unaware of the mission's objective until afterwards, and the CIA and JSOC went to great lengths to ensure that no preparatory or preliminary activities inadvertently breached mission security.

With many months to plan, prepare and practice on a full scale mock-up of the objective, US Navy SEALs, US Army pilots and aircrews for this mission were probably the most repetitively rehearsed and specially trained force in the history of special operations. All of the participants were already the most elite and experienced special operations forces available. The extensive repetition served to ensure they were fully focused and able to react, adapt and succeed under any contingency.

Two further factors were critical. Speed in execution of the mission was prevalent. The mission was planned and rehearsed to be successfully completed with all participants extracted within 30 minutes. This was not only to be in compliance with McRaven's model to attain relative superiority, but also because of the limited fuel and time available to the supporting aircraft. Finally, the principle of purpose (as defined by McRaven as "understanding and executing the prime objective of the mission regardless of emerging obstacles or opportunities") was inherent in every aspect of the mission plan. Every participant fully comprehended the gravity of achieving mission success.

CONCLUSION

The impact of the death of Osama bin Laden was felt immediately, not only in a worldwide response, but also from intelligence material collected from the compound. The captured data revealed much about bin Laden and al-Qaeda. Thousands of electronic exchanges between Bin Laden and his al-Qaeda deputies around the world showed bin Laden urging his own strategy for Afghanistan after America's projected 2014 troop withdrawals. The captured information revealed how bin Laden stayed in touch with the established affiliates of al-Qaeda, and continued to seek new alliances with groups such as Boko Haram in Nigeria. According to these documents, bin Laden sought to reassert control over factions of loosely affiliated jihadists from Yemen to Somalia, as well as independent players whom he believed had sullied al-Qaeda's reputation and muddied his central message. Bin Laden was worried at times about his personal security and was annoyed that his organization had not utilized the Arab Spring to improve its image.

The journalist Joby Warrick, writing in the *Washington Post* on May 1, 2012, assessed bin Laden's actions as those of "a chief executive fully engaged in the group's myriad crises, grappling with financial problems, recruitment, rebellious field managers and sudden staff vacancies resulting from the unrelenting U.S. drone campaign." He was also "a hands-on manager who participated in the terrorist group's operational planning and strategic thinking while also giving orders and advice to field operatives scattered worldwide."

However, other accounts emphatically assert that bin Laden had been relegated out of any control over al-Qaeda assets or operations and was in relative exile and retirement. The truth may be somewhere in between, and it may never be known. Only time can tell of this raid's long term impact. In the end, the mission to kill Osama bin Laden was not as effective toward defeating al-Qaeda or winning the "War on Terrorism," as it was a moral victory and a reckoning. Killing Osama bin Laden could never compensate for the tragedies he imposed, but just the same, as a result of Operation *Neptune Spear*, justice was served.

BIBLIOGRAPHY

Abbottabad Commission Report, Al Jazeera, January 4, 2013. http://www.aljazeera.com/indepth/spotlight/binladenfiles/

Abdel Bari Atwan, *The Secret History of Al Qaeda*, University of California Press, 2008

"Al-Qaeda had warned of Pakistan strike", Asia Times Online, May 27, 2011. http://atimes.com/atimes/South_Asia/ME27Df06.html

Amna Yousaf Khokhar, *Operation Neptune Spear: A Watershed in the War against Terrorism*, Institute of Strategic Studies, 2012

Bassam Javed, "Osama's death closes a chapter", May 08, 2011. http://www.thenews.com.pk

Bergen, Peter L., *Manhunt: The Ten-Year Search for Bin Laden from 9/11 to Abbottabad*, Broadway Books, 2013

Bowden, Mark, *The Finish: The Killing of Osama Bin Laden*, Atlantic Monthly Press, 2012

Cawthorne, Nigel, *Warrior Elite: 31 Heroic Special-Ops Missions from the Raid on Son Tay to the Killing of Osama Bin Laden*, Ulysses Press, 2011

"Ilyas Kashmiri killed in drone strike", *The Express Tribune*, June 4, 2011. http://tribune.com.pk/story/182247/drone-strike-kills-five-in-south-waziristan-officials/

Juergensmeyer, Mark, *Terror in the Mind of God: The Global Rise of Religious Violence*, University of California Press, 2003

Lebovich, Andrew, "Al-Qaeda names Zwahiri new leader", The AfPak Channel, June 16, 2011. http://afpak.foreignpolicy.com/posts/2011/06/16/daily_brief_al_qaeda_names_zawahiri_new_leader

McRaven, Admiral William H., *Spec Ops: Case Studies in Special Operations Warfare: Theory and Practice*, Presidio Press, 2011

Murad Batal al-Shishani, "Understanding Strategic Change in Al-Qaeda's Central Leadership after Bin Laden", *Terrorism Monitor*, Volume IX, Issue 23 (June 9, 2011)

Nemcoff, Mark Yoshimoto, *The Killing of Osama Bin Laden: How the Mission to Hunt Down a Terrorist Mastermind was Accomplished*, Glenneyre Press LLC, 2012

Osama bin Laden: Death in Abbottabad – Official Story of the Navy SEAL Raid into Pakistan, Videos Captured from the Compound, Implications for Future of al Qaeda, Legal and Military Issues (DVD-ROM) Progressive Management, 2011

Owen, Mark and Maurer, Kevin, *No Easy Day: The Firsthand Account of the Mission that Killed Osama bin Laden*, Dutton Penguin Group, NY, 2012

"Pakistani officials knew about Baitullah, Zawahiri meeting", *The Express Tribune*, July 18, 2011. http://tribune.com.pk/story/212025/pakistani-officials-knew-about-baitullah-zawahiri-meeting/

Raman, B., "Bin Laden's Fatwa Against Musharraf and Pakistani Army", Paper No. 284, *International Terrorism Monitor*. http://www.southasiaanalysis.org/papers24/paper2388.html

Rashid, Ahmed, *Descent into Chaos: The US and the Disaster in Pakistan, Afghanistan, and Central Asia*, Penguin, 2009

Pfarrer, Chuck, *SEAL Target Geronimo: The Inside Story of the Mission to Kill Osama Bin Laden*, Quercus, 2011

Schmindle, Nicholas, *"Getting Bin Laden"*, The New Yorker (August 8, 2011)

Smith, Michael, *Killer Elite: The Real Story Behind Seal Team Six and the Bin Laden Raid*, Orion, 2011

Syed Saleem Shahzad, *Inside Al-Qaeda and the Taliban: Beyond Bin Laden and 9/11*, London, Pluto Press, 2011

"The Hunt for Osama Bin Laden", *The New York Times*, December 17, 2012

The Osama bin Laden Files: Letters and Documents Discovered by SEAL Team Six During their Raid on bin Laden's Compound, Skyhorse Publishing, 2012

The Osama bin Laden Mission: Details of the Historic Raid ordered by President Barack Obama, Captured Videos, Navy SEAL Background Information, The Future of al Qaeda, Progressive Management, 2011

ZERO DARK THIRTY, screenplay and research: writer Mark Boal and producer Kathryn Bigelow, Annapurna Pictures, with Columbia and Universal, 2012

INDEX

References to illustrations and plates are shown in **bold**. Captions to plates are shown in brackets.